SELECTED POEMS OF
TENNYSON

THE POETRY BOOKSHELF
General Editor: James Reeves

SELECTED POEMS OF

TENNYSON

Edited with an Introduction
and Notes
by

EDMUND BLUNDEN

HEINEMANN

LONDON

Heinemann Educational Books Ltd

LONDON EDINBURGH MELBOURNE TORONTO

SINGAPORE JOHANNESBURG AUCKLAND

IBADAN HONG KONG NAIROBI

S B N   435   15028   6   (cased edition)
S B N   435   15029   4   (paperback)

ALFRED LORD TENNYSON 1809–1892

INTRODUCTION AND NOTES © EDMUND BLUNDEN 1960

FIRST PUBLISHED 1960
REPRINTED 1962, 1963, 1964, 1968, 1969

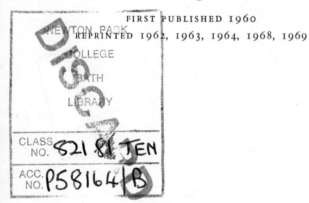
Published by
Heinemann Educational Books Ltd
48 Charles Street, London W1X 8AH
Printed in Great Britain by Morrison & Gibb Ltd
London and Edinburgh

CONTENTS

INTRODUCTION

I

TENNYSON'S POPULARITY
THE THINKER

In 1884 an English writer was made a peer of the realm in recognition of his poetical works. That had not happened before and has not happened since. Alfred Tennyson, who had already declined to accept a baronetcy, but had been Poet Laureate for many years, now did not shun the title of Baron Tennyson of Aldworth and Farringford. Such elevation was not regarded by Victorians, if memory of their outlook serves the present writer, as an extraordinary thing. But then in 1884 Tennyson's fame had already had a long history. That history and its main bias are worth recalling, however briefly.

So far back as 1827 the triumphant poet, then a youth merely, had contributed substantially to a book published at Louth in Lincolnshire, under the title *Poems by Two Brothers* (actually, it was by three of them). It was not at all a 'Kilmarnock Burns', and may have deserved the later verdict of Stopford Brooke: 'Shelley's verses before *Queen Mab* were detestable. Tennyson's verses in the *Poems by Two Brothers* were only not quite so bad.' But three years after the trial volume the case was altered. In 1830 Alfred Tennyson's young friend A. H. Hallam sent a couple of new poetry-books for the favour of a review to the critic who some years earlier had been the first to tell us what shining new poets we had in Shelley and in Keats. The critic, Leigh Hunt, with his singular power of seeing swiftly all coming excellence in literature, did not miss this fresh opportunity.

In serving as herald to Alfred Tennyson, Hunt saw something of the agreeable dilemma which he had known in other days when he found himself, so to say, in charge of the two Young Poets, Keats and Shelley. The books which Arthur Hallam submitted to him came from Two Brothers both meritorious and promising well. Alfred's *Poems, Chiefly Lyrical* and Charles's *Sonnets and Fugitive Pieces* were in a manner competitive. As editor of *The Tatler* Hunt took great pains over his long review, which was printed in four instalments.

The word 'competitive' just now may have puzzled one or two readers of these lines. Of Charles Tennyson possibly few today recollect much more than that when he died, in 1879, Alfred wrote a most affectionate and natural lament for him as a 'true poet'—the brother who once knew and shared all his hopes. Their paths had diverged. Charles had almost gone out of view in the literary field by devoting himself soon enough to the secluded duties of a country clergyman. But in 1830 it was not altogether easy for a reader to pronounce which of the two Tennysons would emerge as *the* poet Tennyson. Leigh Hunt's review opened with that point unsettled, though with inclusive acclamation: 'We have great pleasure in stating that we have seen no such poetical writing since the last volume of Mr. Keats' —Mr. Keats!; 'and that the authors, who are both young men, we believe, at college, may take their stand at once among the first poets of the day. We mean, that Mr. Wordsworth and Mr. Coleridge may give them the right hand of fellowship' . . . Coleridge when applied to did so—a little less exuberantly.

But Hunt was happy in his own way, and the review bearing its several proud allusions to Keats and Shelley at length came to *The Tatler's* award of the first prize. 'We are bound to state that the more closely we have become acquainted with Alfred Tennyson's poems, the more the author has risen upon our admiration. Perhaps we feel ourselves the more inclined to prefer him to Charles, because he seems less disposed to tie himself down to conventional notions—less willing to blink any great question or feeling, and to put up with a consciousness

2

of doing so.' This, we reflect, was written by one of the courageous new poets who had urged Reform early in the century in many directions—by the friend of Shelley with all his devotion to freedom of mind.

Was the opinion valid? There was to be plenty of time in which to examine it in the light of Alfred Tennyson's increasing poetical productions. Now it might be said that Hunt was right and now that he was wrong in attributing an unconventional outlook to his new poet; he must have been perplexed himself sometimes in the succeeding twenty or thirty years. Tennyson could be entrenched and conventional enough on subjects which Reformists had fought over, and Hunt's own eldest son—the clever editor of *The Leader* in which such independent writers as G. H. Lewes were concerned—presently defined him as combining in his poetry too often the clergyman and the magistrate.

But that definition was not adequate; for Tennyson's poems were quite as likely to 'ring out the old' as to resist and condemn change. If that observation is not accepted, yet it will be allowed that this poet of feminine fancy and exquisite artistry was on the whole a studious disputant on great questions or prevalent feelings. The recurrent impulse in him was the necessity of doing what, in his time, Matthew Arnold publicly maintained to be the task of the poet: the 'criticism of life'. To return to Leigh Hunt's criticism and the years before Queen Victoria, Tennyson came out even in his 'pretty' period with such adventurous uses of verse as we find in the sceptical sketch, 'Supposed Confessions of a Second-Rate Sensitive Mind Not in Unity with Itself'. The title, of course, indicates a degree of caution which Lamb's 'Confessions of a Drunkard' does not. But Tennyson's applauded psychological effusion had a stronger sequel when in 1842 he came again into the tiresome arena of criticism with the two volumes of *Poems*, reprinted in 1843.

Leigh Hunt was still in the business, well remembering the author's earlier publication, and once again he investigated

Alfred Tennyson's chances of being the new Keats, Shelley, or thereabouts. The tinkling prettinesses which he had before let pass now drew his censure as 'fantastic nothings', but when he studied the poem 'The Two Voices', which is a sustained study of a suicidal intention and all the considerations which it developed, the critic became entirely Tennyson's partisan. He went so far as to tell England that it was 'a mixture of thought and feeling, more abundant in the former respect than Keats, and more pleasurable and luxuriant in the latter than Wordsworth'.

And still Tennyson had before him decade after decade for the writing of poetry, which was all that he did write for the world at large, and it was as a sort of umpire of thought—among the great thinkers of the Victorian era as well as among the instructed multitude of miscellaneous persons—that he seems to have obtained the deepest veneration all round. Samuel Laurence drew his portrait beautifully soon after the appearance of the *Poems* in 1842, and thereafter declared that Alfred Tennyson struck him as the strongest-minded man he had known; Laurence drew many celebrated men and women. Mr. F. L. Lucas has told us of all the pamphlets which demonstrate the artist's view as afterwards becoming general: what does TENNYSON think, and say, on—more or less anything? Wide as was the variety of his poetical performance, with the accent so much on the loveliness and the serenity of the world, he naturally returned with anxious cogitation (mingled with certain unphilosophical feelings) to the questions worrying the nineteenth century and possibly many other centuries. Romance, fable, daydream and luxury evoked from him a profusion of verbal niceties, metrical innovations. At length the theatre tempted him, the lover of Shakespeare, to write several handsome dramas. In all these lucubrations, and in his very lyrics other than those penned for musicians to set, it was principally the thought that he wished to enthrone. It is recorded that when he

4

was in the company of thinkers Tennyson said little: but he waited, and in solitude questioned, and in some way he answered—'*pro tem*'. '*If* I could understand.' The words are his own. But who ever could, when it was the awkward old poser 'What is Life?'

Many were pleased by Alfred Tennyson's manner in his trains of thought, with their attendant emotional utterances (italicized in his rejection of the evolutionary creed as it was flippantly circulated: 'I was *born* to other things'; in that exclamation the 'I' may have been, like Thomas Hardy's, only a dramatized pronoun). Art played its part, we know. The ideas of Tennyson could never have flowed so far and so easily round the Victorian scene had they been offered in even Coleridgean prose, and unassisted by that current of personal statement which may be an unfair advantage at some points to the poet.

'We can note'—the words are from Mr. John Collier, not Tennyson's most bouquet-minded critic—'in the first years of Victoria's reign, the way in which modern thought became coincident with poetical feeling, and how it was Tennyson who first became conscious of it.' To say this even in few words was to amplify what Tennyson's invaluable son Hallam had told us: 'Scientific leaders like Herschel, Owen, Sedgwick and Tyndall regarded him as a champion of Science.' And such was the chief garland earned in England by the master of language, if not of pure reason, in an age which loved lectures and self-education and great thoughts—the Victorian poets were expected to compete with the Victorian dons and divines.

II

TENNYSON'S EARLY LIFE

Generally, until a few years ago, it was the impression that Tennyson's early life was one of simple rural happiness, but the modern biography by Sir Charles Tennyson with admirable candour denies it. It is not in doubt, of course, that our poet was born at Somersby village near Horncastle in Lincolnshire on 6 August 1809—one of the large family of the Reverend George Clayton Tennyson. This clergyman seems to have fitted Mrs. Gaskell's description of the father of the Brontës rather better than Patrick Brontë himself; more and more he made life at the crowded rectory difficult and gloomy, working off his own disappointments on the members of his household. We are persuaded that his son Alfred, through these early experiences, became inclined towards the morbid mood which often shades his poetry, down to the latest examples. Moreover the boy apparently did not enjoy his time at Louth Grammar School. The sweet influence of his mother (who lived until 1865) has not been contradicted.

There was poetry in the family, and again a comparison with the young, much-composing Brontës at Haworth arises; for the brothers Frederick, Charles, Alfred and Septimus were all versemen at an early period. They were also voracious readers all. Alfred's boyish verses, he later on observed, were ridiculously fluent—his pen could run into hundreds of rhyming couplets, he composed an epic several thousand lines long. Some of these compositions escaped destruction, and one, the extensive dramatic attempt called 'The Devil and the Lady', published in our time, is among the most brilliant of juvenilia by an English writer. At the end of 1826 Charles and Alfred with limited assistance from Frederick, and without any name on their title-page, put forth *Poems by Two Brothers*. The publishers were the bookseller brothers Jackson of Louth; it was quite a substantial volume; and the surviving wonder is that the Jacksons paid the poets £20. Yet the name 'Byron' may have been in their minds; it was a Byronic miscellany, and this fact summons up the detail that in 1824, upon the news of the Childe's untimely death in the struggle for the liberty of Greece, Alfred Tennyson 'walked out alone, and carved, "Byron is dead!" into the sandstone'.

It is not to be forgotten that Lincolnshire includes plenty of noble landscape, thanks in part to that high ground the Wolds, and that the sea was not many miles away from Tennyson's home. As a boy Tennyson learned to contemplate the landscape and the bounding sea, besides all smaller scenery of copse, rivulet, farm and lawn; to this excellent command, visual and affectionate, he could and did return through the years with a softly charming and sometimes a grand effect in poetry. The sea is possibly his poetic image in chief.

The year 1828 saw him (with Charles still beside him) transformed into a Cambridge undergraduate, at Trinity College. It was now that Tennyson met among other high-spirited and able young men a recent hero of the Eton Debating Society, Arthur Henry Hallam, whose father was a celebrated historian. The friendship that followed made literary history. 'Both were poets, both worked together at poetry, both looked forward to a long life of art together.' Say equally a long life of thought; for to such as Tennyson this young Hallam shone forth as a constant inspirer of deep discussion and original and epoch-making 'directions'. We may scarcely discover from Hallam's *Remains* the supremacy which his friends discerned in the living man, and Tennyson above all, who for all his show of character needed a guide and philosopher as well as a friend.

During his first year as an undergraduate Tennyson wrote in blank verse 'The Lover's Tale', which has beauty though no narrative force, and competed successfully for the Chancellor's Medal (1829) with a poetical exercise on the set subject 'Timbuctoo'. Its romantic enthusiasm was such as to remind readers of Shelley and of Keats, if indeed they had yet much awareness of these two, whose reputations were being lifted up at Cambridge. Next came the *Poems Chiefly Lyrical* already spoken of, in 1830, with a second volume in 1832 quite superior to the other—begemmed with things soon accounted precious. Among these were 'The Miller's Daughter' (dear to Queen

Victoria), 'The May Queen', 'The Palace of Art' and 'The Lotus Eaters', all of them in themselves and in their reception revealing that romantic poetry was turning into something else.

Hallam had become engaged to Tennyson's sister Emily, and the whole association, intellectual, imaginative, personal, was advancing agreeably when on 15 September 1833, on a visit to Vienna, Hallam 'was snatched away by sudden death'. The calamity reduced Tennyson to misery and, almost, helplessness. 'He was,' he reflected, 'as near perfection as any mortal man could be'—but without Hallam, what could that do for the slow hours? However, it was possible to find a degree of relief in writing verses with his friend in mind, and some short elegies were soon composed in an uncommon though simple and 'obvious' stanza form, and time went on. He records that his dramatic monologue 'Ulysses' was written soon after Hallam's death—an expression of his 'feelings about the need of going forward and braving the struggle of life'.

Tennyson had resources enough, after his Cambridge days, to live in 'honourable poverty' without a profession, and he had some London years of no great importance except that he made friends with remarkable men of letters. W. M. Thackeray, at that date like him in having to win his spurs, thought him 'the wisest man he had ever met', and Thomas Carlyle, allowing London to support and to be cultivated by him, was for once wholly pleased with a South Briton. He at least sent word to R. W. Emerson in America, 'Alfred is one of the few British and foreign figures who are and remain beautiful to me—a living human soul, to whom your own soul can say, Brother! One of the finest looking men in the world. A great shock of rough, dusty, dark hair; bright, laughing, hazel eyes; massive aquiline face, most massive, yet most delicate; of sallow-brown complexion, almost Indian-looking; clothes cynically loose, free-and-easy; smokes infinite tobacco. His voice is musically metallic—fit for loud laughter and piercing wail, and all that may lie between; speech and speculation free and plenteous; I do not meet, in these late decades, such company over a pipe! We shall see what he will grow to.'

Between 1833 and 1842 the poet hardly troubled to print anything, possibly because the old and still damnatory *Quarterly Review* had treated him much as it had treated Shelley and Keats before. Until 1837 he could still find a roof at Somersby Rectory, though his father had died in 1831, but then he became a wanderer for a time. Among the places where he lived, Epping Forest brought him a curious misfortune. He met at High Beech the proprietor of a private asylum, Dr. Matthew Allen, whose most distinguished patient was John Clare; but Tennyson seems to have missed Clare, and his dealings with Allen were concerned with investing some family funds in Allen's Patent Decorative Carving and Sculpture Company. Allen became a bankrupt in 1843 and all seemed lost: Tennyson had a nervous collapse. However, Dr. Allen died in 1845 and his life insurance more or less covered what Tennyson had lost; besides, in 1845, Sir Robert Peel advised the Queen to give the poet a Civil List Pension of £200.

'Of his powers of imagination and expression,' Peel told Her Majesty, 'many competent judges think most highly.' Indeed, the publication of *Poems* in two volumes in 1842 was a great success. The work was a revision of the earlier productions with numerous noble additions, as titles like 'The Two Voices', 'Morte d'Arthur' and 'Locksley Hall' (to mention no more) soon show. The effect on literary people was illustrated by such notices of Tennyson as a whole chapter in *A New Spirit of the Age*, 1844, edited by R. H. Horne—and in that book the poet's picture engraved after Samuel Laurence was much admired. A slight discord in the sweet tune of growing fame happened when Sir Edward Bulwer Lytton, in an anonymous satire called 'The New Timon', thought fit to ridicule Tennyson's

jingling medley of purloined conceits,
Out-babying Wordsworth and out-glittering Keats.

Over the signature 'Alcibiades' Tennyson retorted vigorously in verse in the pages of *Punch*.

It is better to qualify such disturbances with milder poetic addresses, such as Hartley Coleridge's sonnet 'Visiting the Lakes'. Tennyson had not made himself known to Wordsworth, but the delighted Hartley entertained him well.

TO ALFRED TENNYSON

Long have I known thee as thou art in song,
And long enjoy'd the perfume that exhales
From thy pure soul, and odour sweet entails
And permanence, on thoughts that float along
The stream of life, to join the passive throng
Of shades and echoes that are memory's being
Hearing we hear not, and we see not seeing,
If passion, fancy, faith move not among
The never-present moments of reflection.
Long have I view'd thee in the crystal sphere
Of verse, that, like the beryl, makes appear
Visions of hope, begot of recollection.
Knowing thee now, a real earth-treading man,
Not less I love thee, and no more I can.

The Princess; a Medley, indeed a poetical tract for the times, appeared in 1847 and was well received. But the great moment came when *In Memoriam* offered the reader all those elegies written since 1833 for A. H. Hallam; though the author's name was not given, there was no real mystery. Among the reviewers was Mr. Gladstone who still remembered Hallam and his glorious promise, but now observed that his name would live in connection with this volume. That forecast has been justified. *In Memoriam*, however, even in 1850, was welcomed not simply as a tribute to a particular friend in the world of light, but as a help to seekers after truth, questioners of the eternal will, friends of faith with some recurrent obstacles to it.

The year 1850 must have been an uncommonly emotional one for Tennyson, apart from the fortunate launching of his most important series of verses on the ethical deeps. There were two other great things, his marriage, and his appointment as Poet Laureate in succession to William Wordsworth. His bride was Emily Sellwood of Horncastle in his native county, and she was a niece of the valiant Arctic explorer Sir John Franklin. The fine verses on Franklin's cenotaph in Westminster Abbey are by Tennyson. Concerning the sequel to the poet's wedding at Shiplake in Oxfordshire, a Victorian voice is best: 'Tennyson's married life, unlike that of so many poets, has been one of un-alloyed tenderness and love. . . . But who will dare to lift the veil and inquire too closely into the private life of one who, in conversation with a friend, has said, "I believe that every crime and every vice in the world are connected with the passion for autographs and anecdotes and records; the desiring anecdotes and acquaintance with the lives of great men is treating them like pigs to be ripped open for the public. I know that I myself shall be ripped open like a pig." '

To turn to the Laureateship—Mr. Kenneth Hopkins has chronicled the circumstances of Tennyson's appointment duly in his *Poets Laureate*—one or two possibilities were discussed in 1850; old Samuel Rogers might get it, or rather younger Leigh Hunt, or quite young Elizabeth Barrett (Mrs. Browning). But Lord John Russell wrote to the Prince Consort quite firmly, 'Mr. Tennyson is a fit person to be Poet Laureate,' and Prince Albert and the Queen were already Tennysonians in respect of the poetry itself. 'Generally speaking,' Mr. Hopkins decides, 'he was successful with all his official poems.' It was soon after Tennyson received the laurel that he addressed the Queen in his *In Memoriam* stanza, as he presented his 'poor book of song' to her, with extraordinary ability for such ceremonial yet not unmeaning composition. Then in 1852 the death of the Iron Duke required a poem, and Tennyson's 'Ode', duly issued on the morning of the funeral, though not applauded by every critic, certainly was equal to the occasion on the whole and rich in many of the 'household words' which Tennyson gave to his age.

III

THE LAUREATE

Forty years and several changes of abode now awaited the shy Laureate, who could not evade the penalty of poetical distinction—a bombardment of manuscripts from less admired poets. But if that was the worst of his troubles, Tennyson was as fortunate as poets can be. His income was secure, his books were increasingly in demand. Where would he make his home? In 1853 he chose the western end of Isle of Wight and there presently bought Farringford near Freshwater. After fourteen years he acquired land near Haslemere, there to build a 'refuge'. The South Country evidently took his fancy, in spite of memories of the Lincolnshire wolds.

The University of Oxford had conferred the honorary D.C.L. degree on Wordsworth in 1839; in 1855 it did as much for Tennyson.

Like his predecessor in office, Tennyson was a traveller, and his tours gave him a view of many countries, from Wales to Italy, from Norway to Portugal. In 1860 he wandered in Cornwall with a 'bright, thoughtful friend' named Francis Turner Palgrave, fervent in the new work of national education. The result—or the main result—of this tour was the appearance of a selection called *The Golden Treasury of the Best Songs and Lyrical Poems in the English Language* in 1861. In his dedication to Alfred Tennyson, whose work was not represented only because no living writer was admitted, Palgrave wrote, 'Your encouragement, given me while traversing the wild scenery of Treryn Dinas, led me to begin the work; and it has been completed under your advice and assistance'. In 1897 Palgrave's second series was dedicated to the memory of his supervisor, 'sadly and affectionately', and of its 190 items Tennyson's share was twenty-three.

When we contemplate the immense distribution of that *Golden Treasury* which still continues round the world, these words truly appear laconic, and essential to any account of Tennyson's work.

It was noticed by Miss Caroline Fox of Falmouth when the anthologists on holiday visited her home that Tennyson 'reads the Reviews of his Poems, and is amused to find how often he is misunderstood'. The word 'amused' may be regarded as a kindly choice. In 1855 Tennyson's *Maud*, a spasmodic affair which at all events left to coming generations the drawing-room lyric inviting Maud into the garden, was not received with complete satisfaction. An honorary degree from Oxford University could not altogether bring Tennyson out of a mood of suffering and retreat.

Still, he was constant to an old idea of composing a greater work than *Maud: a Monodrama*, and followed the Romantics in considering the Arthurian legends as a likely theme. It was mentioned that his 1842 volume contained a specimen of what he could do with it, the 'Morte d'Arthur'. The progress of the grand work in his imagination, excellently suited to a Laureate of Britain, was revealed in 1859 by the issue of *Idylls of the King* —four pieces of epic and not so epic poetry. Here at any rate was an occasion which brought acclamations enough to please the author, and wealth besides. At the end of 1861 the Prince Consort died. Tennyson found his hour to associate this excellent man and leader with his enlarged *Idylls* in a splendid dedication:

These to His Memory—since he held them dear,
Perchance as finding there unconsciously
Some image of himself—I dedicate,
I dedicate, I consecrate with tears
These Idylls.
               And indeed He seems to me
Scarce other than my King's ideal knight. . . .

Such elegiac offerings were not unobserved by the royal widow.

The dignity of Tennyson in the national scene thus became assured. Not even Dickens could achieve such an effect, Dickens who was among the most ardent Tennysonians. This status, however, was not purely a triumph of poetry, and behind the scenes some of the Laureate's old friends, the translator of Omar Khayyám for one, demurred concerning the evolution of the wild-wood, early Tennyson into the industrious studio worker.

Enoch Arden, a tale in verse with some resemblance to a line of tales about shipwrecked solitaries (Defoe's, Thomson's, Cowper's, Kirke White's ideas on these mariners were all quite available) came out with other poems in 1864. By that date such psychologically powerful studies in verse as Meredith's *Modern Love* were being talked about, but Tennyson's *Maud* had scarcely made him believe his public wanted that kind of thing from him. *Enoch Arden*, though parodists might snipe, was the thing.

Tennyson's mother lived to see the *Enoch Arden* volume, with its Lincolnshire poems, at once a success, but died in 1865. Still, she had seen in 1864 both her poet-sons of chief note bring out their books, and in Charles's sonnets she might have enjoyed a quiet deep thinking which was becoming difficult for famous Alfred. Frederick Tennyson had published his *Days and Hours* ten years before, and it was nearly a master hand's work—but the final masterdom was missing.

The Poet Laureate had been desired by the Duke of Argyll to do something with the mystical Holy Grail as he extended the Arthurian *Idylls*, and in 1869 the 'Holy Grail' was provided with other additions. The next supplement was the volume (1872) containing 'Gareth and Lynette' and 'The Last Tournament', the second title showing that Tennyson thought the work now written to the end; but thirteen years later these Idylls received their latest reinforcement. Since the 'Morte d'Arthur' in manuscript had been lent to W. S. Landor, to his delight and wonder, in 1837, there can be no doubt of Tennyson's following the gleam through all vicissitudes. What was that gleam? Only some of his poems, that late lyric 'Merlin' for example, can give us an answer, and it is as true as it is untranslatable.

IV

LAST DECADES

As the Romantic poets before him had done, Tennyson attempted to supply the nineteenth-century theatre with poetic dramas in the Elizabethan tradition, and though he was over sixty when he began to make this his business he took a great deal of trouble with it. It was the time when England rejoiced in the gifts of Sir Henry Irving as actor and producer, and it might have been thought that the combination of the Laureate and this extraordinary performer would have been exceedingly successful—in *Queen Mary* for example, which was put on in 1874. Irving took the rôle of Philip II of Spain. But neither *Queen Mary* nor *Becket* (a little luckier) nor any of the other plays which form a sizable section of Tennyson's collected works had natural touches enough to keep the stage long. Even the songs in these plays were of little adult interest or meaning. Enormous speeches abounded, but character was scanty. In 1881 *The Cup* had the benefit of Irving's and of Ellen Terry's acting. *The Promise of May* in 1882 upset some of the public as it appeared 'to associate libertinism with advanced thought', and to condemn honest doubt.

This theatre campaign occupied Tennyson for something like ten years, but he had not forgotten his ordinary poetical occupations, and in 1880 a volume called *Ballads and other Poems* seemed to open a new series of lyrical collections; *Tiresias and other Poems* in 1885 included his last Idyll; *Locksley Hall Sixty Years After* followed and was received with special attention in 1886, *Demeter and other Poems* in 1889, and finally *The Death of Œnone* in 1892.

Meanwhile, among his various travels, Tennyson had been the companion of Mr. Gladstone, then Prime Minister, on a sea trip aboard s.s. *Pembroke Castle* in 1883, and at Copenhagen the two had been visited by the King of Denmark, the Czar and Czarina, and other royal persons. For some reason his friend the Queen of England did not think that this trip was entirely correct conduct, but she accepted the suggestion that Tennyson should become Baron Tennyson of Aldworth and Farringford. Aldworth was the house (designed by the editor of *The Nineteenth Century*, James Knowles) which he had had built in 1867 near Haslemere in the hope of securing privacy, which of course he could not have in one view—the view of the postman. His sufferings from correspondence were great, but then so was his reputation, so was the income that his poems brought him.

In 1884 Tennyson chose Italy for his vacation rambles, with his admirable son Hallam. He was still able to make his occasional little tours when his eightieth years was near; even afterwards. It was on one of these, when Hallam was again his companion, that he had the inspiration from simple experience which was soon expressed with delicate power in 'Crossing the Bar'. It was Hallam's good fortune to be the poem's earliest reader other than its author, and he was in no hesitation over its merit. Set to music, it was for many years familiar to English congregations. The figurative nature of the poem was at one time a puzzle to many of Tennyson's readers, especially the line 'I hope to see my Pilot face to face', concerning the meaning of which a correspondence occurred in *The Times*. Was this Pilot nautically correct? 'So much learning was indeed expended on the inquiry as to where and when the Pilot was first taken on board, that one wonders that none of the correspondents raised the question of his certificate.'

Outliving his main rival in English poetry, Robert Browning, to whom with his 'genius and geniality' he had dedicated the *Tiresias* volume, Tennyson stayed until 6 October 1892. The poet's death, the hand clasping the volume of Shakespeare, the moonlight calm about the room, the sea not far away made one more picture for the general imagination in which he had so long been picturesque. On 12 October he was duly sepulchred in Westminster Abbey. Lady Tennyson survived until 1896.

Perhaps only an inspection of albums containing some of the articles, many of them illustrated, which marked the passing of Tennyson, can now tell us unmistakably how famous he was. The poets were moved to write elegies in profusion. The most noted of them, at that time, was A. C. Swinburne, and he offered his *in memoriam*; the most expected of the younger school, William Watson, lamented the master in the grand manner. But it is enough here to quote some lines from an unusual poet, T. H. Huxley the scientist, who had drawn on Tennyson's poetry in his lectures, and who now imagined Westminster Abbey speaking on 12 October 1892.

> . . . Bring me my dead!
> Into the storied hall,
> Where I have garnered all
> My harvest without weed;
> My chosen fruits of goodly seed;

17

And lay him gently down among
The men of state, the men of song;
The men that would not suffer wrong:
The thought-worn chieftains of the mind:
Head servants of the human kind.

To attempt a collection of personal details about Tennyson
would exasperate his ghost and possibly intervene between his
poetry and ourselves. Some things, however, may be gathered
which illustrate his attitude to life and thus his operations as a
writer. He was inordinately shy, and the handicap of short sight
made this difficulty greater for him. There is the tale of the
popular preacher from Brighton calling on him, a man who
in Victorian days helped to spread Tennyson's ideas. But
at this first call, 'I felt,' the Laureate confessed, 'as if he
had come to pluck out the heart of my mystery—so I talked
to him about nothing but beer.' Alarmed at the prospect of
meeting anybody he did not know, Tennyson nevertheless
believed himself capable of summing up character at a
glance.

It has been briefly noticed that he was inclined to talk about
criticisms of his work when they were not eulogies. 'He never
could forget an unfriendly word, even from the most obscure
and insignificant and unknown quarter.' So, his friend James
Knowles remembered. 'He was hurt by it as a sensitive child
might be hurt by the cross look of a passing stranger. . . . He
knew it was a weakness in him, and could be laughed out of it
for a time, but it soon returned upon him, and had given him
from his early youth exaggerated vexation. When remonstrated
with for the Hogarth's perspective he thus made, he would
grimly smile and say, "oh yes, I know. I'm black-blooded like
all the Tennysons—I remember everything that has been said
against me, and forget all the rest". It was his temperament, and
showed itself in other matters besides criticism. For instance, the
last time I went with him to the oculist, he was most heartily

reassured about his eyes by the great expert after a careful and detailed inspection. But as we left the door he turned to me and said with utter gloom, "No man shall persuade me I'm not going blind".' This melancholia can be traced in much of his poetry, with its wild darknesses (ascribed perhaps to some imaginary personality, but not always).

James Knowles also records Tennyson's fondness for telling 'good stories' over his bottle of port and says that his supply of them was 'marvellous'. It is obvious that a large part of his poetical enterprise lay in the field of narrative, though not of a specially precise or realistic sort. Among the tales he told so well after dinner one was about the alleged adventures of his father as a young man in Russia. George Clayton Tennyson, he believed, had escaped 'after an incautious speech about the recent murder of the Emperor Paul; he wandered for months in the Crimea, where "the wild people of the country came about him" and explained to him that twice a year only, at uncertain times, a courier passed through the place blowing a horn before him, and that then was his only chance of safety; he lay waiting and listening through the nights until the weird sound came'—and so on. It smacks of Munchausen rather than workable history, but the *Idylls* as narratives are not all much more credible.

Tennyson was an independent reader of poetry and other literature, and his comments on what he read are often exciting; they do not pretend to be treatises, but are rather exclamations of a vital enthusiasm. They might be wild shots, sometimes; but they were intended. Not everybody, moreover, who was as deeply concerned with his own work as Tennyson was, is recorded as offering to defray the expenses of an edition or another's work which he looked on as regrettably neglected. This Tennyson did in the same instance of the poet-mathematician George Darley, who will always have his inner ring of devotees.

THINKER AND ARTIST

Among the poems of Thomas Hardy which dwell on the transitory nature of tastes and adorations *An Ancient to Ancients* refers to the apparent indifference to Tennyson's poetry some forty years ago.

> The bower we shrined to Tennyson,
>> Gentlemen,
> Is roof-wrecked; damps there drip upon
> Sagged seats, the creeper-nails are rust,
> The spider is sole denizen;
> Even she who voiced those rhymes is dust,
>> Gentlemen.

There must always be some mortality involved even in a life-work of poetry. But Hardy's picturesque opinion that Tennyson too had yielded to the new order invites us to recollect what Mr. Gladstone said when he was with the poet in 1884 and landing at Kirkwall they were given the freedom of the burgh: 'The Poet Laureate has written his own song on the hearts of his countrymen, that can never die. Time is powerless against him.'

In the first part of this short account of Tennyson, it was suggested that many of his countrymen in his own period esteemed him as one of their thinkers, their teachers; the popularity he enjoyed thus was long ago distinguished from the appreciation of a resourceful artist in an essay by H. D. Traill. 'When, in fact, we talk of Tennyson's "popularity", intending thereby to describe that wide and increasing influence which he exercised for upwards of forty years over the minds of educated Englishmen we are really not speaking of him as a poet at all. Let us not forget that, though to have wielded such a power is a good and a great thing—is, if you like to think so, a better and a greater thing than to have been the greatest of poets—it is not the same thing. . . . It would hardly, I imagine, be misrepresenting them to say that, in their opinion, it is the subject-matter—the religious musings, the philosophical and moral reflections—of *In Memoriam* which insure the poem its immortality, and that it is upon that immortality that Tennyson depends for his own.' The readers thus described would also want the *Idylls of the King* canonized, not for its poetic claims but because King Arthur had been made into a sweet gentleman, 'a type of Christian chivalry'.

The two 'Locksley Hall' poems should be considered not only in their relation to one another but as they were of practical importance to their England, to the thoughtful man who inherited position and means and was looking for counsel from contemporary seers. To us these clangorous pieces are dramatic monologues, yet perhaps even now we pass from them with the sense that we have been listening to a deliberate address on the progress of society. Our forefathers felt that Tennyson was himself delivering his very beliefs through these energetic and sentimental theatralia. In the early poem,

Not in vain the distance beacons. Forward, forward let us range,
Let the great world spin for ever down the ringing grooves of change.
Thro' the shadow of the globe we sweep into the younger day:
Better fifty years of Europe than a cycle of Cathay.

Cathay has since almost illustrated this passion for progress. In the later poem,

Gone the cry of 'Forward, Forward', lost within a growing gloom;
Lost, or only heard in silence from the silence of a tomb.

Half the marvels of my morning, triumphs over time and space,
Staled by frequence, shrunk by usage into commonest commonplace!
'Forward' rang the voices then, and of the many mine was one.
Let us hush this cry of 'Forward' till ten thousand years have gone.

Whatever the quality of the thinking in and round such verses was, the zeal and accent of the reasoner are still able to seize the mind and heart. On these occasions Tennyson brings out a bold and large-figured speech which when it was new and simultaneous with questions of the day quickly worked.

His influence, then, was much the same for many as though he had been a writer of prose works. The prose-writer with whom he was compared and from whom he was judged to have learned certain notions, though now we may not readily see this, was Thomas Carlyle. The same general 'transcendentalism' was discovered in *In Memoriam*, 1850, as in *Sartor Resartus*, 1833: 'There is in man a Higher than Love of Happiness; he can do without Happiness, and instead thereof find Blessedness!' Of *In Memoriam* it may still be said that the reader who cares less for the nameless graces of poetry than for the extricable meanings may endorse the Victorian verdict on it, as the poem of the age. Even now the apparent battle between science and religion may compel us to seek for a sympathetic voice, and Tennyson has that; 'and all is well'. His 'science' is about as much as most of us have today, in spite of the popularizers.

The *Idylls*, it may be thought, furnish an example of inspiration dying when composition begins. Tennyson originally seems to have enjoyed the Arthurian Legend and then a vaguely connected medievalism without particular desire to organize his moments of fancy and honour into a single design. It is not a rare situation in the history of poets, and then the next thing is the heavy vast construction within which the original spark of wonder and delight keeps very few rooms warm. Though the first fruits of Tennyson's Camelot dreams were beautiful and romantic, the entire display—as it seems at the moment—is waxwork. Though Tennyson taught how mansoul achieves celestial light beneath the detailed narrative (which Milton would not, on consideration attempt) not much happens to his reader now; his mighty men and airy-fairy women 'ain't real' and that is the end of it. Still, once the morality was the thing.

Tennyson was compared in his lifetime to Alexander Pope long before him in point of his verbal felicity; the *Essay on Man* was noted for its contribution to the fund of quotation in daily use but *In Memoriam* was very soon as successful a contributor. In this matter of the mastery of language, Tennyson remains something of a puzzle. He often twists the poor language with a mercilessly ingenious touch. But he can be as clear and simple as the Ten Commandments.

> So runs my dream: but what am I?
> An infant crying in the night:
> An infant crying for the light:
> And with no language but a cry.

Nature? Art? The two surely in one. This lucidity may not be the Tennysonian distinction which Victorian admirers were likely to praise profusely; that, which made William Watson in 1892 write

> Master who crown'st our immelodious days
> With flower of perfect speech;

but it belongs to the poems in which he responds as most completely to his inner life and spiritual experience.

To the end of his days, though he set such value on the thing he had to say in his poetry, Tennyson was an ardent explorer of the poetic art, the possibilities of vocabulary and locution, the range of metres and musical sequences of speech. He delighted in his power over words as sounds descriptive of 'the thing itself', and his original audience was delighted by him in this. Whether in fact he was right in regarding

> The mellow lin-lan-lone of evening bells

as his very best line of verse, among so many experiments in imitative verbal music, does not greatly matter. It is desirable that our poets should be Tennysonians in their approach to versification, which always had a kinship with music itself, and can enchant us into an understanding of the deepest intuitions and concepts. This quality is not limited in Tennyson to dove and bell onomatopoeia, by any means; he can handle great metres and strong and emphatic sounds, as in that other line of despair almost, when he sees overshadowing the old legendary hill of Poetry two shapes—

These are Astronomy and Geology, terrible Muses!

Few poets' books offer a wider variety of theme, occasion, mood and form than Tennyson's. Lyrics, ballads, dramatic sketches, allegories and parables, national and international addresses, tributes to the great and good, humorous gossipings, moments of universal conjecture, fancies of golden ages and their chivalry, exercises in the classical style—these and more remain from his long life dominated by a deathless trust in poetry. The critical complaint may still be that Tennyson is not usually able to speak with that natural and pathetic directness of many writers less brilliant—and so, when A. E. Housman came along, it was inevitable that Tennyson should at least for a time seem to be away from the living scene. In truth, for many years before Tennyson wrote his last, many poets were gaining audiences without resembling him much in form, spirit or song. But let us now revert to, say, 'Merlin and the Gleam', and, even with Housman's flight in the company of the silent Mercury over his happy highways and coloured counties in mind, we have from Tennyson without knotted wordings a vision of beauty and wisdom travelling alluringly through the mysterious landscape.

Mariana

'Mariana in the moated grange.'
Measure for Measure.

With blackest moss the flower-plots
   Were thickly crusted, one and all:
The rusted nails fell from the knots
   That held the pear to the gable-wall.
The broken sheds look'd sad and strange:
   Unlifted was the clinking latch;
   Weeded and worn the ancient thatch
Upon the lonely moated grange.
     She only said, 'My life is dreary,
       He cometh not,' she said;   10
     She said, 'I am aweary, aweary,
       I would that I were dead!'

Her tears fell with the dews at even;
   Her tears fell ere the dews were dried;
She could not look on the sweet heaven,
   Either at morn or eventide.
After the flitting of the bats,
   When thickest dark did trance the sky,
   She drew her casement-curtain by,
And glanced athwart the glooming flats.   20
     She only said, 'The night is dreary,
       He cometh not,' she said;
     She said, 'I am aweary, aweary,
       I would that I were dead!'

Upon the middle of the night,
 Waking she heard the night-fowl crow:
The cock sung out an hour ere light:
 From the dark fen the oxen's low
Came to her: without hope of change,
 In sleep she seem'd to walk forlorn,   30
 Till cold winds woke the gray-eyed morn
About the lonely moated grange.
  She only said, 'The day is dreary,
   He cometh not,' she said;
  She said, 'I am aweary, aweary,
   I would that I were dead!'

About a stone-cast from the wall
 A sluice with blacken'd waters slept,
And o'er it many, round and small,
 The cluster'd marish-mosses crept.   40
Hard by a poplar shook alway,
 All silver-green with gnarled bark:
 For leagues no other tree did mark
The level waste, the rounding gray.
  She only said, 'My life is dreary,
   He cometh not,' she said;
  She said, 'I am aweary, aweary,
   I would that I were dead!'

And ever when the moon was low,
 And the shrill winds were up and away, 50
In the white curtain, to and fro,
 She saw the gusty shadow sway.
But when the moon was very low,
 And wild winds bound within their cell,
 The shadow of the poplar fell
Upon her bed, across her brow.

She only said, 'The night is dreary,
  He cometh not,' she said;
She said, 'I am aweary, aweary,
  I would that I were dead!'   60

All day within the dreamy house,
  The doors upon their hinges creak'd;
The blue fly sung in the pane; the mouse
  Behind the mouldering wainscot shriek'd,
Or from the crevice peer'd about.
  Old faces glimmer'd thro' the doors,
  Old footsteps trod the upper floors,
Old voices called her from without.
  She only said, 'My life is dreary,
    He cometh not,' she said;   70
  She said, 'I am aweary, aweary,
    I would that I were dead!'

The sparrow's chirrup on the roof,
  The slow clock ticking, and the sound
Which to the wooing wind aloof
  The poplar made, did all confound
Her sense; but most she loathed the hour
  When the thick-moted sunbeam lay
  Athwart the chambers, and the day
Was sloping toward his western bower.   80
  Then, said she, 'I am very dreary,
    He will not come,' she said;
  She wept, 'I am aweary, aweary,
    Oh God, that I were dead!'

Ode to Memory

Addressed to ——

I

Thou who stealest fire,
From the fountains of the past,
To glorify the present; oh, haste,
    Visit my low desire!
Strengthen me, enlighten me!
I faint in this obscurity,
Thou dewy dawn of memory.

II

Come not as thou camest of late,
  Flinging the gloom of yesternight
On the white day; but robed in soften'd light
    Of orient state.
Whilome thou camest with the morning mist,
  Even as a maid, whose stately brow
The dew-impearled winds of dawn have kiss'd,
    When, she, as thou,
Stays on her floating locks the lovely freight
Of overflowing blooms, and earliest shoots
Of orient green, giving safe pledge of fruits,
Which in wintertide shall star
The black earth with brilliance rare.

III

Whilome thou camest with the morning mist,
  And with the evening cloud,

Showering thy gleaned wealth into my open breast
(Those peerless flowers which in the rudest wind
       Never grow sere,
When rooted in the garden of the mind,
  Because they are the earliest of the year).
      Nor was the night thy shroud.
In sweet dreams softer than unbroken rest
Thou leddest by the hand thine infant Hope.   30
The eddying of her garments caught from thee
The light of thy great presence; and the cope
  Of the half-attain'd futurity,
  Tho' deep not fathomless,
Was cloven with the million stars which tremble
O'er the deep mind of dauntless infancy.
Small thought was there of life's distress;
For sure she deem'd no mist of earth could dull
Those spirit-thrilling eyes so keen and beautiful:
Sure she was nigher to heaven's spheres,   40
Listening the lordly music flowing from
      The illimitable years.
  O strengthen me, enlighten me!
  I faint in this obscurity,
  Thou dewy dawn of memory.

IV

Come forth, I charge thee, arise,
Thou of the many tongues, the myriad eyes!
Thou comest not with shows of flaunting vines
      Unto mine inner eye,
      Divinest Memory!   50
  Thou wert not nursed by the waterfall
Which ever sounds and shines
  A pillar of white light upon the wall

Of purple cliffs, aloof descried:
Come from the woods that belt the gray hill-side,
The seven elms, the poplars four
That stand beside my father's door,
And chiefly from the brook that loves
To purl o'er matted cress and ribbed sand,
Or dimple in the dark of rushy coves,   60
Drawing into his narrow earthen urn,
    In every elbow and turn,
The filter'd tribute of the rough woodland,
    O! hither lead thy feet!
Pour round mine ears the livelong bleat
Of the thick-fleeced sheep from wattled folds,
    Upon the ridged wolds,
When the first matin-song hath waken'd loud
Over the dark dewy earth forlorn,
    What time the amber morn   70
Forth gushes from beneath a low-hung cloud.

v

Large dowries doth the raptured eye
  To the young spirit present
    When first she is wed;
      And like a bride of old
    In triumph led,
      With music and sweet showers
      Of festal flowers,
Unto the dwelling she must sway.
Well hast thou done, great artist Memory,   80
  In setting round thy first experiment
    With royal frame-work of wrought gold;
Needs must thou dearly love thy first essay,
And foremost in thy various gallery

Place it, where sweetest sunlight falls
Upon the storied walls;
        For the discovery
And newness of thine art so pleased thee,
That all which thou hast drawn of fairest
    Or boldest since, but lightly weighs   90
With thee unto the love thou bearest
The first-born of thy genius.   Artist-like,
Ever retiring thou dost gaze
On the prime labour of thine early days:
No matter what the sketch might be;
Whether the high field on the bushless Pike,
Or even a sand-built ridge
Of heaped hills that mound the sea,
Overblown with murmurs harsh,
Or even a lowly cottage whence we see   100
Stretch'd wide and wild the waste enormous marsh,
Where from the frequent bridge,
Like emblems of infinity,
The trenched waters run from sky to sky;
Or a garden bower'd close
With plaited alleys of the trailing rose,
Long alleys falling down to twilight grots,
Or opening upon level plots
Of crowned lilies, standing near
Purple-spiked lavender: 110
Whither in after life retired
From brawling storms,
From weary wind,
With youthful fancy re-inspired,
        We may hold converse with all forms
Of the many-sided mind,
And those whom passion hath not blinded,
Subtle-thoughted, myriad-minded.

My friend, with you to live alone,
Were how much better than to own   120
A crown, a sceptre, and a throne!

O strengthen me, enlighten me!
I faint in this obscurity,
Thou dewy dawn of memory.

The Lady of Shalott

PART I

On either side the river lie
Long fields of barley and of rye,
That clothe the wold and meet the sky;
And thro' the field the road runs by
  To many-tower'd Camelot;
And up and down the people go,
Gazing where the lilies blow
Round an island there below,
  The island of Shalott.

Willows whiten, aspens quiver,   10
Little breezes dusk and shiver
Thro' the wave that runs for ever
By the island in the river
  Flowing down to Camelot.
Four gray walls, and four gray towers,
Overlook a space of flowers,
And the silent isle imbowers
  The Lady of Shalott.

By the margin, willow-veil'd,
Slide the heavy barges trail'd   20

By slow horses; and unhail'd
The shallop flitteth silken-sail'd
      Skimming down to Camelot:
But who hath seen her wave her hand?
Or at the casement seen her stand?
Or is she known in all the land,
      The Lady of Shalott?

Only reapers, reaping early
In among the bearded barley,
Hear a song that echoes cheerly   30
From the river winding clearly,
      Down to tower'd Camelot:
And by the moon the reaper weary,
Piling sheaves in uplands airy,
Listening, whispers ''Tis the fairy
      Lady of Shalott.'

PART II

There she weaves by night and day
A magic web with colours gay.
She has heard a whisper say,
A curse is on her if she stay   40
      To look down to Camelot.
She knows not what the curse may be,
And so she weaveth steadily,
And little other care hath she,
      The Lady of Shalott.

And moving thro' a mirror clear
That hangs before her all the year,
Shadows of the world appear.
There she sees the highway near
      Winding down to Camelot: 50

There the river eddy whirls,
And there the surly village-churls,
And the red cloaks of market girls,
        Pass onward from Shalott.

Sometimes a troop of damsels glad,
An abbot on an ambling pad,
Sometimes a curly shepherd-lad,
Or long-hair'd page in crimson clad,
        Goes by to tower'd Camelot;
And sometimes thro' the mirror blue   60
The knights come riding two and two:
She hath no loyal knight and true,
        The Lady of Shalott.

But in her web she still delights
To weave the mirror's magic sights,
For often thro' the silent nights
A funeral, with plumes and lights
        And music, went to Camelot:
Or when the moon was overhead,
Came two young lovers lately wed;   70
'I am half sick of shadows,' said
        The Lady of Shalott.

PART III

A bow-shot from her bower-eaves,
He rode between the barley-sheaves,
The sun came dazzling thro' the leaves,
And flamed upon the brazen greaves
        Of bold Sir Lancelot.
A red-cross knight for ever kneel'd
To a lady in his shield,

That sparkled on the yellow field,
    Beside remote Shalott.

The gemmy bridle glitter'd free,
Like to some branch of stars we see
Hung in the golden Galaxy.
The bridle bells rang merrily
    As he rode down to Camelot:
And from his blazon'd baldric slung
A mighty silver bugle hung,
And as he rode his armour rung,
    Beside remote Shalott.

All in the blue unclouded weather
Thick-jewell'd shone the saddle-leather,
The helmet and the helmet-feather
Burn'd like one burning flame together,
    As he rode down to Camelot.
As often thro' the purple night,
Below the starry clusters bright,
Some bearded meteor, trailing light,
    Moves over still Shalott.

His broad clear brow in sunlight glow'd;
On burnish'd hooves his war-horse trode;
From underneath his helmet flow'd
His coal-black curls as on he rode,
    As he rode down to Camelot.
From the bank and from the river
He flash'd into the crystal mirror,
' Tirra lirra,' by the river
    Sang Sir Lancelot.

She left the web, she left the loom,
She made three paces thro' the room,

She saw the water-lily bloom,
She saw the helmet and the plume,
      She look'd down to Camelot.
Out flew the web and floated wide;
The mirror crack'd from side to side;
'The curse is come upon me,' cried
      The Lady of Shalott.

PART IV

In the stormy east-wind straining,
The pale yellow woods were waning,
The broad stream in his banks complaining,   120
Heavily the low sky raining
      Over tower'd Camelot;
Down she came and found a boat
Beneath a willow left afloat,
And round about the prow she wrote
      The Lady of Shalott.

And down the river's dim expanse
Like some bold seër in a trance,
Seeing all his own mischance—
With a glassy countenance   130
      Did she look to Camelot.
And at the closing of the day
She loosed the chain, and down she lay;
The broad stream bore her far away,
      The Lady of Shalott.

Lying, robed in snowy white
That loosely flew to left and right—
The leaves upon her falling light—
Thro' the noises of the night
      She floated down to Camelot: 140

And as the boat-head wound along
The willowy hills and fields among,
They heard her singing her last song,
    The Lady of Shalott.

Heard a carol, mournful, holy,
Chanted loudly, chanted lowly,
Till her blood was frozen slowly,
And her eyes were darken'd wholly,
    Turn'd to tower'd Camelot.
For ere she reach'd upon the tide   150
The first house by the water-side,
Singing in her song she died,
    The Lady of Shalott.

Under tower and balcony,
By garden-wall and gallery,
A gleaming shape she floated by,
Dead-pale between the houses high,
    Silent into Camelot.
Out upon the wharfs they came,
Knight and burgher, lord and dame,   160
And round the prow they read her name,
    The Lady of Shalott.

Who is this? and what is here?
And in the lighted palace near
Died the sound of royal cheer;
And they cross'd themselves for fear,
    All the knights at Camelot;
But Lancelot mused a little space;
He said, 'She has a lovely face;
God in his mercy lend her grace,   170
    The Lady of Shalott.'

The Two Voices

A still small voice spake unto me,
'Thou art so full of misery,
Were it not better not to be?'

Then to the still small voice I said;
'Let me not cast in endless shade
What is so wonderfully made.'

To which the voice did urge reply;
'To-day I saw the dragon-fly
Come from the wells where he did lie.

'An inner impulse rent the veil   10
Of his old husk: from head to tail
Came out clear plates of sapphire mail.

'He dried his wings: like gauze they grew;
Thro' crofts and pastures wet with dew
A living flash of light he flew.'

I said, 'When first the world began,
Young Nature thro' five cycles ran,
And in the sixth she moulded man.

'She gave him mind, the lordliest
Proportion, and, above the rest,   20
Dominion in the head and breast.'

Thereto the silent voice replied;
'Self-blinded are you by your pride:
Look up thro' night: the world is wide.

'This truth within thy mind rehearse,
That in a boundless universe
Is boundless better, boundless worse.

'Think you this mould of hopes and fears
Could find no statelier than his peers
In yonder hundred million spheres?'   30

It spake, moreover, in my mind:
'Tho' thou wert scatter'd to the wind,
Yet is there plenty of the kind.'

Then did my response clearer fall:
'No compound of this earthly ball
Is like another, all in all.'

To which he answer'd scoffingly;
'Good soul! suppose I grant it thee,
Who'll weep for thy deficiency?

'Or will one beam be less intense,   40
When thy peculiar difference
Is cancell'd in the world of sense?'

I would have said, 'Thou canst not know,'
But my full heart, that work'd below,
Rain'd thro' my sight its overflow.

Again the voice spake unto me:
'Thou art so steep'd in misery,
Surely 'twere better not to be.

39

'Thine anguish will not let thee sleep,
Nor any train of reason keep:
Thou canst not think, but thou wilt weep.'

I said, 'The years with change advance:
If I make dark my countenance,
I shut my life from happier chance.

'Some turn this sickness yet might take,
Ev'n yet.' But he: 'What drug can make
A wither'd palsy cease to shake?'

I wept, 'Tho' I should die, I know
That all about the thorn will blow
In tufts of rosy-tinted snow;

'And men, thro' novel spheres of thought
Still moving after truth long sought,
Will learn new things when I am not.'

'Yet,' said the secret voice, 'some time,
Sooner or later, will gray prime
Make thy grass hoar with early rime.

'Not less swift souls that yearn for light,
Rapt after heaven's starry flight,
Would sweep the tracts of day and night.

'Not less the bee would range her cells,
The furzy prickle fire the dells,
The foxglove cluster dappled bells.'

I said that 'all the years invent;
Each month is various to present
The world with some development.

'Were this not well, to bide mine hour,
Tho' watching from a ruin'd tower
How grows the day of human power?'

'The highest-mounted mind,' he said,
'Still sees the sacred morning spread
The silent summit overhead.

'Will thirty seasons render plain
Those lonely lights that still remain,
Just breaking over land and main?

'Or make that morn, from his cold crown
And crystal silence creeping down,
Flood with full daylight glebe and town?

'Forerun thy peers, thy time, and let
Thy feet, millenniums hence, be set
In midst of knowledge, dream'd not yet.

'Thou hast not gain'd a real height,
Nor art thou nearer to the light,
Because the scale is infinite.

' 'Twere better not to breathe or speak,
Than cry for strength, remaining weak,
And seem to find, but still to seek.

'Moreover, but to seem to find
Asks what thou lackest, thought resign'd,
A healthy frame, a quiet mind.'

I said, 'When I am gone away,
"He dared not tarry," men will say,
Doing dishonour to my clay.'

'This is more vile,' he made reply,
'To breathe and loathe, to live and sigh,
Than once from dread of pain to die.

'Sick art thou—a divided will
Still heaping on the fear of ill
The fear of men, a coward still.

'Do men love thee? Art thou so bound
To men, that how thy name may sound   110
Will vex thee lying underground?

'The memory of the wither'd leaf
In endless time is scarce more brief
Than of the garner'd Autumn-sheaf.

'Go, vexed Spirit, sleep in trust;
The right ear, that is fill'd with dust,
Hears little of the false or just.'

'Hard task, to pluck resolve,' I cried,
'From emptiness and the waste wide
Of that abyss, or scornful pride!   120

'Nay—rather yet that I could raise
One hope that warm'd me in the days
While still I yearn'd for human praise.

'When, wide in soul and bold of tongue,
Among the tents I paused and sung,
The distant battle flash'd and rung.

'I sung the joyful Pæan clear,
And, sitting, burnish'd without fear
The brand, the buckler, and the spear—

'Waiting to strive a happy strife,   130
To war with falsehood to the knife,
And not to lose the good of life—

'Some hidden principle to move,
To put together, part and prove,
And mete the bounds of hate and love—

'As far as might be, to carve out
Free space for every human doubt,
That the whole mind might orb about—

'To search thro' all I felt or saw,
The springs of life, the depths of awe,   140
And reach the law within the law:

'At least, not rotting like a weed,
But, having sown some generous seed,
Fruitful of further thought and deed,

'To pass, when Life her light withdraws,
Not void of righteous self-applause,
Nor in a merely selfish cause—

'In some good cause, not in mine own,
To perish, wept for, honour'd, known,
And like a warrior overthrown;   150

'Whose eyes are dim with glorious tears,
When, soil'd with noble dust, he hears
His country's war-song thrill his ears:

'Then dying of a mortal stroke,
What time the foeman's line is broke,
And all the war is roll'd in smoke.'

'Yea!' said the voice, 'thy dream was good,
While thou abodest in the bud.
It was the stirring of the blood.

'If Nature put not forth her power   160
About the opening of the flower,
Who is it that could live an hour?

'Then comes the check, the change, the fall,
Pain rises up, old pleasures pall.
There is one remedy for all.

'Yet hadst thou, thro' enduring pain,
Link'd month to month with such a chain
Of knitted purport, all were vain.

'Thou hadst not between death and birth
Dissolved the riddle of the earth.   170
So were thy labour little-worth.

'That men with knowledge merely play'd,
I told thee—hardly nigher made,
Tho' scaling slow from grade to grade;

'Much less this dreamer, deaf and blind,
Named man, may hope some truth to find,
That bears relation to the mind.

'For every worm beneath the moon
Draws different threads, and late and soon
Spins, toiling out his own cocoon.   180

'Cry, faint not: either Truth is born
Beyond the polar gleam forlorn,
Or in the gateways of the morn.

'Cry, faint not, climb: the summits slope
Beyond the furthest flights of hope,
Wrapt in dense cloud from base to cope.

'Sometimes a little corner shines,
As over rainy mist inclines
A gleaming crag with belts of pines.

'I will go forward, sayest thou,   190
I shall not fail to find her now.
Look up, the fold is on her brow.

'If straight thy track, or if oblique,
Thou know'st not. Shadows thou dost strike,
Embracing cloud, Ixion-like;

'And owning but a little more
Than beasts, abidest lame and poor,
Calling thyself a little lower

'Than angels. Cease to wail and brawl!
Why inch by inch to darkness crawl?   200
There is one remedy for all.'

'O dull, one-sided voice,' said I,
'Wilt thou make everything a lie,
To flatter me that I may die?

'I know that age to age succeeds,
Blowing a noise of tongues and deeds,
A dust of systems and of creeds.

'I cannot hide that some have striven,
Achieving calm, to whom was given
The joy that mixes man with Heaven: 210

'Who, rowing hard against the stream,
Saw distant gates of Eden gleam,
And did not dream it was a dream;

'But heard, by secret transport led,
Ev'n in the charnels of the dead,
The murmur of the fountain-head—

'Which did accomplish their desire,
Bore and forebore, and did not tire,
Like Stephen, an unquenched fire.

'He heeded not reviling tones,   220
Nor sold his heart to idle moans,
Tho' cursed and scorn'd, and bruised with stones:

'But looking upward, full of grace,
He pray'd, and from a happy place
God's glory smote him on the face.'

The sullen answer slid betwixt:
'Not that the grounds of hope were fix'd,
The elements were kindlier mix'd.'

I said, 'I toil beneath the curse,
But, knowing not the universe,   230
I fear to slide from bad to worse.

'And that, in seeking to undo
One riddle, and to find the true,
I knit a hundred others new:

'Or that this anguish fleeting hence,
Unmanacled from bonds of sense,
Be fix'd and froz'n to permanence:

46

'For I go, weak from suffering here:
Naked I go, and void of cheer:
What is it that I may not fear?'   240

'Consider well,' the voice replied,
'His face, that two hours since hath died;
Wilt thou find passion, pain or pride?

'Will he obey when one commands?
Or answer should one press his hands?
He answers not, nor understands.

'His palms are folded on his breast:
There is no other thing express'd
But long disquiet merged in rest.

'His lips are very mild and meek: 250
Tho' one should smite him on the cheek,
And on the mouth, he will not speak.

'His little daughter, whose sweet face
He kiss'd, taking his last embrace,
Becomes dishonour to her race—

'His sons grow up that bear his name,
Some grow to honour, some to shame,—
But he is chill to praise or blame.

'He will not hear the north-wind rave,
Nor, moaning, household shelter crave   260
From winter rains that beat his grave.

'High up the vapours fold and swim:
About him broods the twilight dim:
The place he knew forgetteth him.'

'If all be dark, vague voice,' I said,
'These things are wrapt in doubt and dread,
Nor canst thou show the dead are dead.

'The sap dries up: the plant declines.
A deeper tale my heart divines.
Know I not Death? the outward signs?   27

'I found him when my years were few;
A shadow on the graves I knew,
And darkness in the village yew.

'From grave to grave the shadow crept:
In her still place the morning wept:
Touch'd by his feet the daisy slept.

'The simple senses crown'd his head:
"Omega! thou art Lord," they said,
"We find no motion in the dead."

'Why, if man rot in dreamless ease,   28
Should that plain fact, as taught by these,
Not make him sure that he shall cease?

'Who forged that other influence,
That heat of inward evidence,
By which he doubts against the sense?

'He owns the fatal gift of eyes,
That read his spirit blindly wise,
Not simple as a thing that dies.

'Here sits he shaping wings to fly:
His heart forebodes a mystery: 29
He names the name Eternity.

'That type of Perfect in his mind
In Nature can he nowhere find.
He sows himself on every wind.

'He seems to hear a Heavenly Friend,
And thro' thick veils to apprehend
A labour working to an end.

'The end and the beginning vex
His reason: many things perplex,
With motions, checks, and counterchecks.   300

'He knows a baseness in his blood
At such strange war with something good,
He may not do the thing he would.

'Heaven opens inward, chasms yawn,
Vast images in glimmering dawn,
Half shown, are broken and withdrawn.

'Ah! sure within him and without,
Could his dark wisdom find it out,
There must be answer to his doubt,

'But thou canst answer not again.   310
With thine own weapon art thou slain,
Or thou wilt answer but in vain.

'The doubt would rest, I dare not solve.
In the same circle we revolve.
Assurance only breeds resolve.'

As when a billow, blown against,
Falls back, the voice with which I fenced
A little ceased, but recommenced.

'Where wert thou when thy father play'd
In his free field, and pastime made,   320
A merry boy in sun and shade?

'A merry boy they call'd him then,
He sat upon the knees of men
In days that never come again.

'Before the little ducts began
To feed thy bones with lime, and ran
Their course, till thou wert also man:

'Who took a wife, who rear'd his race,
Whose wrinkles gather'd on his face,
Whose troubles number with his days: 330

'A life of nothings, nothing-worth,
From that first nothing ere his birth
To that last nothing under earth!'

'These words,' I said, 'are like the rest;
No certain clearness, but at best
A vague suspicion of the breast:

'But if I grant, thou mightst defend
The thesis which thy words intend—
That to begin implies to end;

'Yet how should I for certain hold,   340
Because my memory is so cold,
That I first was in human mould?

'I cannot make this matter plain,
But I would shoot, howe'er in vain,
A random arrow from the brain.

'It may be that no life is found,
Which only to one engine bound
Falls off, but cycles always round.

'As old mythologies relate,
Some draught of Lethe might await   350
The slipping thro' from state to state.

'As here we find in trances, men
Forget the dream that happens then,
Until they fall in trance again.

'So might we, if our state were such
As one before, remember much,
For those two likes might meet and touch.

'But, if I lapsed from nobler place,
Some legend of a fallen race
Alone might hint of my disgrace;   360

'Some vague emotion of delight
In gazing up an Alpine height,
Some yearning toward the lamps of night;

'Or if thro' lower lives I came—
Tho' all experience past became
Consolidate in mind and frame—

'I might forget my weaker lot;
For is not our first year forgot?
The haunts of memory echo not.

'And men, whose reason long was blind,   370
From cells of madness unconfined,
Oft lose whole years of darker mind.

51

'Much more, if first I floated free,
As naked essence, must I be
Incompetent of memory:

'For memory dealing but with time,
And he with matter, could she climb
Beyond her own material prime?

'Moreover, something is or seems,
That touches me with mystic gleams,   380
Like glimpses of forgotten dreams—

'Of something felt, like something here;
Of something done, I know not where;
Such as no language may declare.'

The still voice laugh'd. 'I talk,' said he,
'Not with thy dreams. Suffice it thee
Thy pain is a reality.'

'But thou,' said I, 'hast missed thy mark,
Who sought'st to wreck my mortal ark,
By making all the horizon dark.   390

'Why not set forth, if I should do
This rashness, that which might ensue
With this old soul in organs new?

'Whatever crazy sorrow saith,
No life that breathes with human breath
Has ever truly long'd for death.

' 'Tis life, whereof our nerves are scant,
Oh life, not death, for which we pant;
More life, and fuller, that I want.'

I ceased, and sat as one forlorn.   400
Then said the voice, in quiet scorn,
'Behold, it is the Sabbath morn.'

And I arose, and I released
The casement, and the light increased
With freshness in the dawning east.

Like soften'd airs that blowing steal,
When meres begin to uncongeal,
The sweet church bells began to peal.

On to God's house the people prest:
Passing the place where each must rest,   410
Each enter'd like a welcome guest.

One walk'd between his wife and child,
With measured footfall firm and mild,
And now and then he gravely smiled.

The prudent partner of his blood
Lean'd on him, faithful, gentle, good,
Wearing the rose of womanhood.

And in their double love secure,
The little maiden walk'd demure,
Pacing with downward eyelids pure.   420

These three made unity so sweet,
My frozen heart began to beat,
Remembering its ancient heat.

I blest them, and they wander'd on:
I spoke, but answer came there none:
The dull and bitter voice was gone.

A second voice was at mine ear,
A little whisper silver-clear,
A murmur, 'Be of better cheer.'

As from some blissful neighbourhood,   430
A notice faintly understood,
'I see the end, and know the good.'

A little hint to solace woe,
A hint, a whisper breathing low,
'I may not speak of what I know.'

Like an Æolian harp that wakes
No certain air, but overtakes
Far thought with music that it makes:

Such seem'd the whisper at my side:
'What is it thou knowest, sweet voice?' I cried.   440
'A hidden hope,' the voice replied:

So heavenly-toned, that in that hour
From out my sullen heart a power
Broke, like the rainbow from the shower,

To feel, altho' no tongue can prove,
That every cloud, that spreads above
And veileth love, itself is love.

And forth into the fields I went,
And Nature's living motion lent
The pulse of hope to discontent.   450

I wonder'd at the bounteous hours,
The slow result of winter showers:
You scarce could see the grass for flowers.

I wonder'd, while I paced along:
The woods were fill'd so full with song,
There seem'd no room for sense of wrong;

And all so variously wrought,
I marvell'd how the mind was brought
To anchor by one gloomy thought;

And wherefore rather I made choice   460
To commune with that barren voice,
Than him that said, 'Rejoice! Rejoice!'

The Lotos-Eaters

'Courage!' he said, and pointed toward the land,
'This mounting wave will roll us shoreward soon.'
In the afternoon they came unto a land
In which it seemed always afternoon.
All round the coast the languid air did swoon,
Breathing like one that hath a weary dream.
Full-faced above the valley stood the moon;
And like a downward smoke, the slender stream
Along the cliff to fall and pause and fall did seem.

A land of streams! some, like a downward smoke,   10
Slow-dropping veils of thinnest lawn, did go;
And some thro' wavering lights and shadows broke,
Rolling a slumbrous sheet of foam below.
They saw the gleaming river seaward flow
From the inner land: far off, three mountain-tops

Three silent pinnacles of aged snow,
Stood sunset-flush'd: and, dew'd with showery drops,
Up-clomb the shadowy pine above the woven copse.

The charmed sunset linger'd low adown
In the red West: thro' mountain clefts the dale   20
Was seen far inland, and the yellow down
Border'd with palm, and many a winding vale
And meadow, set with slender galingale;
A land where all things always seem'd the same!
And round about the keel with faces pale,
Dark faces pale against that rosy flame,
The mild-eyed melancholy Lotos-eaters came.

Branches they bore of that enchanted stem,
Laden with flower and fruit, whereof they gave
To each, but whoso did receive of them,   30
And taste, to him the gushing of the wave
Far far away did seem to mourn and rave
On alien shores; and if his fellow spake,
His voice was thin, as voices from the grave;
And deep-asleep he seem'd, yet all awake,
And music in his ears his beating heart did make.

They sat them down upon the yellow sand,
Between the sun and moon upon the shore;
And sweet it was to dream of Fatherland,
Of child, and wife, and slave; but evermore   40
Most weary seem'd the sea, weary the oar,
Weary the wandering fields of barren foam.
Then some one said, 'We will return no more;'
And all at once they sang, 'Our island home
Is far beyond the wave; we will no longer roam.'

Choric Song

I

There is sweet music here that softer falls
Than petals from blown roses on the grass,
Or night-dews on still waters between walls
Of shadowy granite, in a gleaming pass;
Music that gentlier on the spirit lies,   50
Than tir'd eyelids upon tir'd eyes;
Music that brings sweet sleep down from the blissful skies.
Here are cool mosses deep,
And thro' the moss the ivies creep,
And in the stream the long-leaved flowers weep,
And from the craggy ledge the poppy hangs in sleep.

II

Why are we weigh'd upon with heaviness,
And utterly consumed with sharp distress,
While all things else have rest from weariness?
All things have rest: why should we toil alone,   60
We only toil, who are the first of things,
And make perpetual moan,
Still from one sorrow to another thrown:
Nor ever fold our wings,
And cease from wanderings,
Nor steep our brows in slumber's holy balm;
Nor harken what the inner spirit sings,
'There is no joy but calm!'
Why should we only toil, the roof and crown of things?

III

Lo! in the middle of the wood,   70
The folded leaf is woo'd from out the bud

With winds upon the branch, and there
Grows green and broad, and takes no care,
Sun-steep'd at noon, and in the moon
Nightly dew-fed; and turning yellow
Falls, and floats adown the air.
Lo! sweeten'd with the summer light,
The full-juiced apple, waxing over-mellow,
Drops in a silent autumn night.
All its allotted length of days, 80
The flower ripens in its place,
Ripens and fades, and falls, and hath no toil,
Fast-rooted in the fruitful soil.

IV

Hateful is the dark-blue sky,
Vaulted o'er the dark-blue sea.
Death is the end of life; ah, why
Should life all labour be?
Let us alone. Time driveth onward fast,
And in a little while our lips are dumb.
Let us alone. What is it that will last? 90
All things are taken from us, and become
Portions and parcels of the dreadful Past.
Let us alone. What pleasure can we have
To war with evil? Is there any peace
In ever climbing up the climbing wave?
All things have rest, and ripen toward the grave
In silence; ripen, fall and cease:
Give us long rest or death, dark death, or dreamful ease.

V

How sweet it were, hearing the downward stream,
With half-shut eyes ever to seem 100
Falling asleep in a half-dream!

To dream and dream, like yonder amber light,
Which will not leave the myrrh-bush on the height;
To hear each other's whisper'd speech;
Eating the Lotos day by day,
To watch the crisping ripples on the beach,
And tender curving lines of creamy spray;
To lend our hearts and spirits wholly
To the influence of mild-minded melancholy;
To muse and brood and live again in memory,   110
With those old faces of our infancy
Heap'd over with a mound of grass,
Two handfuls of white dust, shut in an urn of brass!

VI

Dear is the memory of our wedded lives,
And dear the last embraces of our wives
And their warm tears: but all hath suffer'd change:
For surely now our household hearths are cold:
Our sons inherit us: our looks are strange:
And we should come like ghosts to trouble joy.
Or else the island princes over-bold   120
Have eat our substance, and the minstrel sings
Before them of the ten years' war in Troy,
And our great deeds, as half-forgotten things.
Is there confusion in the little isle?
Let what is broken so remain.
The Gods are hard to reconcile:
'Tis hard to settle order once again.
There *is* confusion worse than death,
Trouble on trouble, pain on pain,
Long labour unto aged breath,   130
Sore task to hearts worn out by many wars
And eyes grown dim with gazing on the pilot-stars.

VII

But, propt on beds of amaranth and moly,
How sweet (while warm airs lull us, blowing lowly)
With half-dropt eyelid still,
Beneath a heaven dark and holy,
To watch the long bright river drawing slowly
His waters from the purple hill—
To hear the dewy echoes calling
From cave to cave thro' the thick-twined vine—   140
To watch the emerald-colour'd water falling
Thro' many a wov'n acanthus-wreath divine!
Only to hear and see the far-off sparkling brine,
Only to hear were sweet, stretch'd out beneath the pine.

VIII

The Lotos blooms below the barren peak:
The Lotos blows by every winding creek:
All day the wind breathes low with mellower tone:
Thro' every hollow cave and alley lone
Round and round the spicy downs the yellow Lotos-
    dust is blown.
We have had enough of action, and of motion we,   150
Roll'd to starboard, roll'd to larboard, when the surge
    was seething free,
Where the wallowing monster spouted his foam-fountains
    in the sea.
Let us swear an oath, and keep it with an equal mind,
In the hollow Lotos-land to live and lie reclined
On the hills like Gods together, careless of mankind.
For they lie beside their nectar, and the bolts are hurl'd
Far below them in the valleys, and the clouds are lightly
    curl'd
Round their golden houses, girdled with the gleaming
    world:

Where they smile in secret, looking over wasted lands,
Blight and famine, plague and earthquake, roaring deeps and fiery sands, 160
Clanging fights, and flaming towns, and sinking ships, and praying hands.
But they smile, they find a music centred in a doleful song
Steaming up, a lamentation and an ancient tale of wrong,
Like a tale of little meaning tho' the words are strong;
Chanted from an ill-used race of men that cleave the soil,
Sow the seed, and reap the harvest with enduring toil,
Storing yearly little dues of wheat, and wine and oil;
Till they perish and they suffer—some, 'tis whisper'd—down in hell
Suffer endless anguish, others in Elysian valleys dwell,
Resting weary limbs at last on beds of asphodel. 170
Surely, surely, slumber is more sweet than toil, the shore
Than labour in the deep mid-ocean, wind and wave and oar;
Oh rest ye, brother mariners, we will not wander more.

Of Old Sat Freedom

Of old sat Freedom on the heights,
    The thunders breaking at her feet:
Above her shook the starry lights:
    She heard the torrents meet.

There in her place she did rejoice,
    Self-gather'd in her prophet-mind,
But fragments of her mighty voice
    Came rolling on the wind.

Then stept she down thro' town and field
    To mingle with the human race,   10
And part by part to men reveal'd
    The fullness of her face—

Grave mother of majestic works,
    From her isle-altar gazing down,
Who, God-like, grasps the triple forks,
    And, King-like, wears the crown:

Her open eyes desire the truth.
    The wisdom of a thousand years
Is in them. May perpetual youth
    Keep dry their light from tears;   20

That her fair form may stand and shine,
    Make bright our days and light our dreams,
Turning to scorn with lips divine
    The falsehood of extremes!

Morte D'Arthur

So all day long the noise of battle roll'd
Among the mountains by the winter sea;
Until King Arthur's table, man by man,
Had fallen in Lyonnesse about their Lord,
King Arthur: then, because his wound was deep,
The bold Sir Bedivere uplifted him,
Sir Bedivere, the last of all his knights,
And bore him to a chapel nigh the field,
A broken chancel with a broken cross,

That stood on a dark strait of barren land. 10
On one side lay the Ocean, and on one
Lay a great water, and the moon was full.
    Then spake King Arthur to Sir Bedivere:
'The sequel of to-day unsolders all
The goodliest fellowship of famous knights
Whereof this world holds record. Such a sleep
They sleep—the men I loved. I think that we
Shall never more, at any future time,
Delight our souls with talk of knightly deeds,
Walking about the gardens and the halls   20
Of Camelot, as in the days that were.
I perish by this people which I made,—
Tho' Merlin sware that I should come again
To rule once more—but let what will be, be
I am so deeply smitten thro' the helm
That without help I cannot last till morn.
Thou therefore take my brand Excalibur,
Which was my pride: for thou rememberest how
In those old days, one summer noon, an arm
Rose up from out the bosom of the lake,   30
Clothed in white samite, mystic, wonderful,
Holding the sword—and how I row'd across
And took it, and have worn it, like a king:
And, wheresoever I am sung or told
In aftertime, this also shall be known:
But now delay not: take Excalibur,
And fling him far into the middle mere:
Watch what thou seëst, and lightly bring me word.'
    To him replied the bold Sir Bedivere:
'It is not meet, Sir King, to leave thee thus,   40
Aidless, alone, and smitten thro' the helm.
A little thing may harm a wounded man.
Yet I thy hest will all perform at full,

Watch what I see, and lightly bring thee word.'
  So saying, from the ruin'd shrine he stept
And in the moon athwart the place of tombs,
Where lay the mighty bones of ancient men,
Old knights, and over them the sea-wind sang
Shrill, chill, with flakes of foam. He, stepping down
By zig-zag paths, and juts of pointed rock,   50
Came on the shining levels of the lake.
  There drew he forth the brand Excalibur,
And o'er him, drawing it, the winter moon,
Brightening the skirts of a long cloud, ran forth
And sparkled keen with frost against the hilt:
For all the haft twinkled with diamond sparks,
Myriads of topaz-lights, and jacinth-work
Of subtlest jewellery. He gazed so long
That both his eyes were dazzled, as he stood,
This way and that dividing the swift mind,   60
In act to throw: but at the last it seem'd
Better to leave Excalibur conceal'd
There in the many-knotted waterflags,
That whistled stiff and dry about the marge.
So strode he back slow to the wounded King.
  Then spake King Arthur to Sir Bedivere:
'Hast thou perform'd my mission which I gave?
What is it thou hast seen? or what hast heard?'
  And answer made the bold Sir Bedivere:
'I heard the ripple washing in the reeds,   70
And the wild water lapping on the crag.'
  To whom replied King Arthur, faint and pale:
'Thou hast betray'd thy nature and thy name,
Not rendering true answer, as beseem'd
Thy fëalty, nor like a noble knight:
For surer sign had follow'd, either hand,
Or voice, or else a motion of the mere.

This is a shameful thing for men to lie.
Yet now, I charge thee, quickly go again
As thou art lief and dear, and do the thing   80
I bad thee, watch, and lightly bring me word.'
    Then went Sir Bedivere the second time
Across the ridge, and paced beside the mere,
Counting the dewy pebbles, fix'd in thought;
But when he saw the wonder of the hilt,
How curiously and strangely chased, he smote
His palms together, and he cried aloud,
    'And if indeed I cast the brand away,
Surely a precious thing, one worthy note,
Should thus be lost for ever from the earth,   90
Which might have pleased the eyes of many men.
What good should follow this, if this were done?
What harm, undone? deep harm to disobey,
Seeing obedience is the bond of rule.
Were it well to obey then, if a king demand
An act unprofitable, against himself?
The King is sick, and knows not what he does.
What record, or what relic of my lord
Should be to aftertime, but empty breath
And rumours of a doubt? but were this kept,   100
Stored in some treasure-house of mighty kings,
Some one might show it at a joust of arms,
Saying, "King Arthur's sword, Excalibur,
Wrought by the lonely maiden of the Lake.
Nine years she wrought it, sitting in the deeps
Upon the hidden bases of the hills."
So might some old man speak in the aftertime
To all the people, winning reverence.
But now much honour and much fame were lost.'
    So spake he, clouded with his own conceit,   110
And hid Excalibur the second time,

And so strode back slow to the wounded King.
    Then spoke King Arthur, breathing heavily:
'What is it thou hast seen? or what hast heard?'
    And answer made the bold Sir Bedivere:
'I heard the water lapping on the crag,
And the long ripple washing in the reeds.'
    To whom replied King Arthur, much in wrath:
'Ah, miserable and unkind, untrue,
Unknightly, traitor-hearted! Woe is me!   120
Authority forgets a dying king,
Laid widow'd of the power in his eye
That bow'd the will. I see thee what thou art,
For thou, the latest-left of all my knights,
In whom should meet the offices of all,
Thou wouldst betray me for the precious hilt;
Either from lust of gold, or like a girl
Valuing the giddy pleasure of the eyes.
Yet, for a man may fail in duty twice,
And the third time may prosper, get thee hence: 130
But, if thou spare to fling Excalibur,
I will arise and slay thee with my hands.'
    Then quickly rose Sir Bedivere, and ran,
And, leaping down the ridges lightly, plunged
Among the bulrush-beds, and clutch'd the sword,
And strongly wheel'd and threw it. The great brand
Made lightnings in the splendour of the moon,
And flashing round and round, and whirl'd in an arch,
Shot like a streamer of the northern morn,
Seen where the moving isles of winter shock   140
By night, with noises of the northern sea.
So flash'd and fell the brand Excalibur:
But ere he dipt the surface, rose an arm
Clothed in white samite, mystic, wonderful,
And caught him by the hilt, and brandish'd him

66

Three times, and drew him under in the mere.)—
And lightly went the other to the King.
    Then spoke King Arthur, drawing thicker breath:
'Now see I by thine eyes that this is done.
Speak out: what is it thou hast heard, or seen?'   150
    And answer made the bold Sir Bedivere:
'Sir King, I closed mine eyelids, lest the gems
Should blind my purpose, for I never saw,
Nor shall see, here or elsewhere, till I die,
Not tho' I live three lives of mortal men,
So great a miracle as yonder hilt.
Then with both hands I flung him, wheeling him;
But when I look'd again, behold an arm,
Clothed in white samite, mystic, wonderful,
That caught him by the hilt, and brandish'd him   160
Three times, and drew him under in the mere.'
    And answer made King Arthur, breathing hard:
'My end draws nigh; 'tis time that I were gone.
Make broad thy shoulders to receive my weight,
And bear me to the margin; yet I fear
My wound hath taken cold, and I shall die.'
    So saying, from the pavement he half rose,
Slowly, with pain, reclining on his arm,
And looking wistfully with wide blue eyes
As in a picture. Him Sir Bedivere   170
Remorsefully regarded thro' his tears,
And would have spoken, but he found not words,
Then took with care, and kneeling on one knee,
O'er both his shoulders drew the languid hands,
And rising bore him thro' the place of tombs.
    But, as he walk'd, King Arthur panted hard,
Like one that feels a nightmare on his bed
When all the house is mute. So sigh'd the King,
Muttering and murmuring at his ear, 'Quick, quick!

I fear it is too late, and I shall die.'
But the other swiftly strode from ridge to ridge,
Clothed with his breath, and looking, as he walk'd,.
Larger than human on the frozen hills.
He heard the deep behind him, and a cry
Before. His own thought drove him, like a goad.
Dry clash'd his harness in the icy caves
And barren chasms, and all to left and right
The bare black cliff clang'd round him, as he based
His feet on juts of slippery crag that rang
Sharp-smitten with the dint of armed heels—   190
And on a sudden, lo! the level lake,
And the long glories of the winter moon.

Then saw they how there hove a dusky barge,
Dark as a funeral scarf from stem to stern,
Beneath them; and descending they were ware
That all the decks were dense with stately forms
Black-stoled, black-hooded, like a dream—by these
Three Queens with crowns of gold—and from them rose
A cry that shiver'd to the tingling stars,
And, as it were one voice an agony   200
Of lamentation, like a wind, that shrills
All night in a waste land, where no one comes,
Or hath come, since the making of the world.

Then murmur'd Arthur, 'Place me in the barge,'
And to the barge they came. There those three Queens
Put forth their hands, and took the King, and wept.
But she, that rose the tallest of them all
And fairest, laid his head upon her lap,
And loosed the shatter'd casque, and chafed his hands,
And call'd him by his name, complaining loud,   210
And dropping bitter tears against his brow
Striped with dark blood: for all his face was white
And colourless, and like the wither'd moon

Smote by the fresh beam of the springing east;
And all his greaves and cuisses dash'd with drops
Of onset; and the light and lustrous curls—
That made his forehead like a rising sun
High from the daïs-throne—were parch'd with dust;
Or, clotted into points and hanging loose,
Mix'd with the knightly growth that fringed his lips.   220
So like a shatter'd column lay the King;
Not like that Arthur who, with lance in rest,
From spur to plume a star of tournament,
Shot thro' the lists at Camelot, and charged
Before the eyes of ladies and of kings.

   Then loudly cried the bold Sir Bedivere,
'Ah! my Lord Arthur, whither shall I go?
Where shall I hide my forehead and my eyes?
For now I see the true old times are dead,
When every morning brought a noble chance,   230
And every chance brought out a noble knight.
Such times have been not since the light that led
The holy Elders with the gift of myrrh.
But now the whole ROUND TABLE is dissolved
Which was an image of the mighty world;
And I, the last, go forth companionless,
And the days darken round me, and the years,
Among new men, strange faces, other minds.'

   And slowly answered Arthur from the barge:
'The old order changeth, yielding place to new,   240
And God fulfils Himself in many ways,
Lest one good custom should corrupt the world.
Comfort thyself: what comfort is in me?
I have lived my life, and that which I have done
May He within Himself make pure! but thou,
If thou shouldst never see my face again,
Pray for my soul. More things are wrought by prayer

Than this world dreams of. Wherefore, let thy voice
Rise like a fountain for me night and day.
For what are men better than sheep or goats. 250
That nourish a blind life within the brain,
If, knowing God, they lift not hands of prayer
Both for themselves and those who call them friend?
For so the whole round earth is every way
Bound by gold chains about the feet of God.
But now farewell. I am going a long way
With these thou seëst—if indeed I go—
(For all my mind is clouded with a doubt)
To the island-valley of Avilion;
Where falls not hail, or rain, or any snow, 260
Nor ever wind blows loudly; but it lies
Deep-meadow'd, happy, fair with orchard-lawns
And bowery hollows crown'd with summer sea,
Where I will heal me of my grievous wound.'
    So said he, and the barge with oar and sail
Moved from the brink, like some full-breasted swan
That, fluting a wild carol ere her death,
Ruffles her pure cold plume, and takes the flood
With swarthy webs. Long stood Sir Bedivere
Revolving many memories, till the hull 270
Look'd one black dot against the verge of dawn,
And on the mere the wailing died away.

Ulysses

It little profits that an idle king,
By this still hearth, among these barren crags,
Match'd with an aged wife, I mete and dole
Unequal laws unto a savage race,

That hoard, and sleep, and feed, and know not me.
I cannot rest from travel: I will drink
Life to the lees: all times I have enjoy'd
Greatly, have suffer'd greatly, both with those
That loved me, and alone; on shore, and when
Thro' scudding drifts the rain Hyades   10
Vext the dim sea: I am become a name;
For always roaming with a hungry heart
Much have I seen and known; cities of men
And manners, climates, councils, governments,
Myself not least, but honour'd of them all;
And drunk delight of battle with my peers,
Far on the ringing plains of windy Troy.
I am a part of all that I have met;
Yet all experience is an arch wherethro'
Gleams that untravell'd world, whose margin fades   20
For ever and for ever when I move.
How dull it is to pause, to make an end,
To rust unburnish'd, not to shine in use!
As tho' to breathe were life. Life piled on life
Were all too little, and of one to me
Little remains: but every hour is saved
From that eternal silence, something more,
A bringer of new things; and vile it were
For some three suns to store and hoard myself,
And this gray spirit yearning in desire   30
To follow knowledge like a sinking star,
Beyond the utmost bound of human thought.

    This is my son, mine own Telemachus,
To whom I leave the sceptre and the isle—
Well-loved of me, discerning to fulfil
This labour, by slow prudence to make mild
A rugged people, and thro' soft degrees
Subdue them to the useful and the good.

71

Most blameless is he, centred in the sphere
Of common duties, decent not to fail   40
In offices of tenderness, and pay
Meet adoration to my household gods,
When I am gone. He works his work, I mine.
   There lies the port; the vessel puffs her sail:
There gloom the dark broad seas. My mariners,
Souls that have toil'd, and wrought, and thought with me—
That ever with a frolic welcome took
The thunder and the sunshine, and opposed
Free hearts, free foreheads—you and I are old;
Old age hath yet his honour and his toil;   50
Death closes all: but something ere the end,
Some work of noble note, may yet be done,
Not unbecoming men that strove with Gods.
The lights begin to twinkle from the rocks:
The long day wanes: the slow moon climbs: the deep
Moans round with many voices. Come, my friends,
'Tis not too late to seek a newer world.
Push off, and sitting well in order smite
The sounding furrows; for my purpose holds
To sail beyond the sunset, and the baths   60
Of all the western stars, until I die.
It may be that the gulfs will wash us down:
It may be we shall touch the Happy Isles,
And see the great Achilles, whom we knew.
Tho' much is taken, much abides; and tho'
We are not now that strength which in old days
Moved earth and heaven; that which we are, we are;
One equal temper of heroic hearts,
Made weak by time and fate, but strong in will
To strive, to seek, to find, and not to yield.   70

Tithonus

The woods decay, the woods decay and fall,
The vapours weep their burthen to the ground,
Man comes and tills the field and lies beneath,
And after many a summer dies the swan.
Me only cruel immortality
Consumes: I wither slowly in thine arms,
Here at the quiet limit of the world,
A white-hair'd shadow roaming like a dream
The ever-silent spaces of the East,
Far-folded mists, and gleaming halls of morn.   10

Alas! for this gray shadow, once a man—
So glorious in his beauty and thy choice,
Who madest him thy chosen, that he seem'd
To his great heart none other than a God!
I ask'd thee, 'Give me immortality.'
Then didst thou grant mine asking with a smile,
Like wealthy men who care not how they give.
But thy strong Hours indignant work'd their wills,
And beat me down and marr'd and wasted me,
And tho' they could not end me, left me maim'd   20
To dwell in presence of immortal youth,
Immortal age beside immortal youth,
And all I was, in ashes. Can thy love,
Thy beauty, make amends, tho' even now,
Close over us, the silver star, thy guide,
Shines in those tremulous eyes that fill with tears
To hear me? Let me go: take back thy gift:

Why should a man desire in any way
To vary from the kindly race of men,
Or pass beyond the goal of ordinance   30
Where all should pause, as is most meet for all?

A soft air fans the cloud apart; there comes
A glimpse of that dark world where I was born.
Once more the old mysterious glimmer steals
From thy pure brows, and from thy shoulders pure,
And bosom beating with a heart renew'd.
Thy cheek begins to redden thro' the gloom,
Thy sweet eyes brighten slowly close to mine,
Ere yet they blind the stars, and the wild team
Which love thee, yearning for thy yoke, arise,   40
And shake the darkness from their loosen'd manes,
And beat the twilight into flakes of fire.

Lo! ever thus thou growest beautiful
In silence, then before thine answer given
Departest, and thy tears are on my cheek.

Why wilt thou ever scare me with thy tears,
And make me tremble lest a saying learnt,
In days far-off, on that dark earth, be true?
'The Gods themselves cannot recall their gifts.'

Ay me! ay me! with what another heart   50
In days far-off, and with what other eyes
I used to watch—if I be he that watch'd—
The lucid outline forming round thee; saw
The dim curls kindle into sunny rings;
Changed with thy mystic change, and felt my blood
Glow with the glow that slowly crimson'd all
Thy presence and thy portals, while I lay,

Mouth, forehead, eyelids, growing dewy-warm
With kisses balmier than half-opening buds
Of April, and could hear the lips that kiss'd   60
Whispering I knew not what of wild and sweet,
Like that strange song I heard Apollo sing,
While Ilion like a mist rose into towers.

Yet hold me not for ever in thine East:
How can my nature longer mix with thine?
Coldly thy rosy shadows bathe me, cold
Are all thy lights, and cold my wrinkled feet
Upon thy glimmering thresholds, when the steam
Floats up from those dim fields about the homes
Of happy men that have the power to die,   70
And grassy barrows of the happier dead.
Release me, and restore me to the ground;
Thou seëst all things, thou wilt see my grave:
Thou wilt renew thy beauty morn by morn;
I earth in earth forget these empty courts,
And thee returning on thy silver wheels.

Locksley Hall

Comrades, leave me here a little, while as yet 'tis early morn:
Leave me here, and when you want me, sound upon the
    bugle-horn.

'Tis the place, and all around it, as of old, the curlews call,
Dreary gleams about the moorland flying over Locksley Hall;

Locksley Hall, that in the distance overlooks the sandy tracts,
And the hollow ocean-ridges roaring into cataracts.

Many a night from yonder ivied casement, ere I went to rest,
Did I look on great Orion sloping slowly to the West.

Many a night I saw the Pleiads, rising thro' the mellow shade,
Glitter like a swarm of fire-flies tangled in a silver braid.　　10

Here about the beach I wander'd, nourishing a youth sublime
With the fairy tales of science, and the long result of Time;

When the centuries behind me like a fruitful land reposed;
When I clung to all the present for the promise that it closed:

When I dipt into the future far as human eye could see;
Saw the Vision of the world, and all the wonder that would
　　　be.——

In the Spring a fuller crimson comes upon the robin's breast;
In the Spring the wanton lapwing gets himself another crest;

In the Spring a livelier iris changes on the burnish'd dove;
In the Spring a young man's fancy lightly turns to thoughts
　　　of love.　　20

Then her cheek was pale and thinner than should be for one
　　　so young,
And her eyes on all my motions with a mute observance hung.

And I said, 'My cousin Amy, speak, and speak the truth to me,
Trust me, cousin, all the current of my being sets to thee.'

On her pallid cheek and forehead came a colour and a light,
As I have seen the rosy red flushing in the northern night.

And she turn'd—her bosom shaken with a sudden storm of
　　　sighs—
All the spirit deeply dawning in the dark of hazel eyes—

Saying, 'I have hid my feelings, fearing they should do me
 wrong;'
Saying, 'Dost thou love me, cousin?' weeping, 'I have loved
 thee long.'   30

Love took up the glass of Time, and turn'd it in his glowing
 hands;
Every moment, lightly shaken, ran itself in golden sands.

Love took up the harp of Life, and smote on all the chords
 with might;
Smote the chord of Self, that, trembling, pass'd in music out
 of sight.

Many a morning on the moorland did we hear the copses
 ring,
And her whisper throng'd my pulses with the fullness of the
 Spring.

Many an evening by the waters did we watch the stately
 ships,
And our spirits rush'd together at the touching of the lips.

O my cousin, shallow-hearted! O my Amy, mine no more!
O the dreary, dreary moorland! O the barren, barren shore! 40

Falser than all fancy fathoms, falser than all songs have sung,
Puppet to a father's threat, and servile to a shrewish tongue!

Is it well to wish thee happy?—having known me—to decline
On a range of lower feelings and a narrower heart than mine!

Yet it shall be: thou shalt lower to his level day by day,
What is fine within thee growing coarse to sympathise with
 clay.

As the husband is, the wife is: thou art mated with a clown,
And the grossness of his nature will have weight to drag thee
    down.

He will hold thee, when his passion shall have spent its novel
    force,
Something better than his dog, a little dearer than his horse. 50

What is this? his eyes are heavy: think not they are glazed
    with wine.
Go to him: it is thy duty: kiss him: take his hand in thine.

It may be my lord is weary, that his brain is overwrought:
Soothe him with thy finer fancies, touch him with thy lighter
    thought.

He will answer to the purpose, easy things to understand—
Better thou wert dead before me, tho' I slew thee with my
    hand!

Better thou and I were lying, hidden from the heart's disgrace,
Roll'd in one another's arms, and silent in a last embrace.

Cursed be the social wants that sin against the strength of
    youth!
Cursed be the social lies that warp us from the living truth! 60

Cursed be the sickly forms that err from honest Nature's rule!
Cursed be the gold that gilds the straiten'd forehead of the
    fool!

Well—'tis well that I should bluster!—Hadst thou less un-
    worthy proved—
Would to God—for I had loved thee more than ever wife
    was loved.

Am I mad, that I should cherish that which bears but bitter
   fruit?
I will pluck it from my bosom, tho' my heart be at the root.

Never, tho' my mortal summers to such length of years
   should come
As the many-winter'd crow that leads the clanging rookery
   home.

Where is comfort? in division of the records of the mind?
Can I part her from herself, and love her, as I knew her, kind? 70

I remember one that perish'd: sweetly did she speak and move:
Such a one do I remember, whom to look at was to love.

Can I think of her as dead, and love her for the love she bore?
No—she never loved me truly: love is love for evermore.

Comfort? comfort scorn'd of devils! this is truth the poet
   sings,
That a sorrow's crown of sorrow is remembering happier
   things.

Drug thy memories, lest thou learn it, lest thy heart be put
   to proof,
In the dead unhappy night, and when the rain is on the roof.

Like a dog, he hunts in dreams, and thou art staring at the
   wall,
Where the dying night-lamp flickers, and the shadows rise
   and fall.   80

Then a hand shall pass before thee, pointing to his drunken
   sleep,

To thy widow'd marriage-pillows, to the tears that thou wilt
    weep.

Thou shalt hear the 'Never, never,' whisper'd by the phantom
    years,
And a song from out the distance in the ringing of thine ears;

And an eye shall vex thee, looking ancient kindness on thy
    pain.
Turn thee, turn thee on thy pillow: get thee to thy rest again.

Nay, but Nature brings thee solace; for a tender voice will
    cry.
'Tis a purer life than thine; a lip to drain thy trouble dry.

Baby lips will laugh me down: my latest rival brings thee
    rest.
Baby fingers, waxen touches, press me from the mother's
    breast.   9

O, the child too clothes the father with a dearness not his due.
Half is thine and half is his: it will be worthy of the two.

O, I see thee old and formal, fitted to thy petty part,
With a little hoard of maxims preaching down a daughter's
    heart.

'They were dangerous guides the feelings—she herself was
    not exempt—
Truly, she herself had suffer'd'—Perish in thy self-contempt!

Overlive it—lower yet—be happy! wherefore should I care?
I myself must mix with action, lest I wither by despair.

What is that which I should turn to, lighting upon days like
    these?
Every door is barr'd with gold, and opens but to golden keys. 100

Every gate is throng'd with suitors, all the markets overflow.
I have but an angry fancy: what is that which I should do?

I had been content to perish, falling on the foeman's ground,
When the ranks are roll'd in vapour, and the winds are laid
    with sound.

But the jingling of the guinea helps the hurt that Honour
    feels,
And the nations do but murmur, snarling at each other's
    heels.

Can I but relive in sadness? I will turn that earlier page.
Hide me from my deep emotion, O thou wondrous Mother-
    Age!

Make me feel the wild pulsation that I felt before the strife,
When I heard my days before me, and the tumult of my
    life; 110

Yearning for the large excitement that the coming years
    would yield,
Eager-hearted as a boy when first he leaves his father's field,

And at night along the dusky highway near and nearer
    drawn,
Sees in heaven the light of London flaring like a dreary
    dawn;

And his spirit leaps within him to be gone before him then,
Underneath the light he looks at, in among the throngs of
    men:

Men, my brothers, men the workers, ever reaping something
    new:
That which they have done but earnest of the things that they
    shall do:

For I dipt into the future, far as human eye could see,
Saw the Vision of the world, and all the wonder that would
    be;   120

Saw the heavens fill with commerce, argosies of magic sails,
Pilots of the purple twilight, dropping down with costly
    bales;

Heard the heavens fill with shouting, and there rain'd a
    ghastly dew
From the nations' airy navies grappling in the central blue;

Far along the world-wide whisper of the south-wind rushing
    warm,
With the standards of the peoples plunging thro' the thunder-
    storm;

Till the war-drum throbb'd no longer, and the battle-flags
    were furl'd
In the Parliament of man, the Federation of the world.

There the common sense of most shall hold a fretful realm
    in awe,
And the kindly earth shall slumber, lapt in universal law.   130

So I triumph'd ere my passion sweeping thro' me left me dry,
Left me with the palsied heart, and left me with the jaundiced
    eye;

Eye, to which all order festers, all things here are out of joint:
Science moves, but slowly slowly, creeping on from point
     to point:

Slowly comes a hungry people, as a lion creeping nigher,
Glares at one that nods and winks behind a slowly-dying fire.

Yet I doubt not thro' the ages one increasing purpose runs,
And the thoughts of men are widen'd with the process of the
     suns.

What is that to him that reaps not harvest of his youthful
     joys,
Tho' the deep heart of existence beat for ever like a boy's? 140

Knowledge comes, but wisdom lingers, and I linger on the
     shore,
And the individual withers, and the world is more and more.

Knowledge comes, but wisdom lingers, and he bears a laden
     breast,
Full of sad experience, moving toward the stillness of his
     rest.

Hark, my merry comrades call me, sounding on the bugle-
     horn,
They to whom my foolish passion were a target for their
     scorn:

Shall it not be scorn to me to harp on such a moulder'd
     string?
I am shamed thro' all my nature to have loved so slight a
     thing.

Weakness to be wroth with weakness! woman's pleasure, woman's pain—
Nature made them blinder motions bounded in a shallower brain: 150

Woman is the lesser man, and all thy passions, match'd with mine,
Are as moonlight unto sunlight, and as water unto wine—

Here at last, where nature sickens, nothing. Ah, for some retreat
Deep in yonder shining Orient, where my life began to beat;

Where in wild Mahratta-battle fell my father evil-starr'd;—
I was left a trampled orphan, and a selfish uncle's ward.

Or to burst all links of habit—there to wander far away,
On from island unto island at the gateways of the day.

Larger constellations burning, mellow moons and happy skies,
Breadths of tropic shade and palms in cluster, knots of Paradise. 160

Never comes the trader, never floats an European flag,
Slides the bird o'er lustrous woodland, swings the trailer from the crag;

Droops the heavy-blossom'd bower, hangs the heavy-fruited tree—
Summer isles of Eden lying in dark-purple spheres of sea.

There methinks would be enjoyment more than in this march of mind,

In the steamship, in the railway, in the thoughts that shake
   mankind.

There the passions cramp'd no longer shall have scope and
   breathing space;
I will take some savage woman, she shall rear my dusky race.

Iron-jointed, supple-sinew'd, they shall dive, and they shall
   run,
Catch the wild goat by the hair, and hurl their lances in the
   sun;   170

Whistle back the parrot's call, and leap the rainbows of the
   brooks,
Not with blinded eyesight poring over miserable books—

Fool, again the dream, the fancy! but I *know* my words are
   wild,
But I count the gray barbarian lower than the Christian
   child.

I, to herd with narrow foreheads, vacant of our glorious
   gains,
Like a beast with lower pleasures, like a beast with lower
   pains!

Mated with a squalid savage—what to me were sun or
   clime?
I the heir of all the ages, in the foremost files of time—

I that rather held it better men should perish one by one,
Than that earth should stand at gaze like Joshua's moon in
   Ajalon !   180

Not in vain the distance beacons. Forward, forward let us range,
Let the great world spin for ever down the ringing grooves of change.

Thro' the shadow of the globe we sweep into the younger day:
Better fifty years of Europe than a cycle of Cathay.

Mother-Age (for mine I knew not) help me as when life begun:
Rift the hills, and roll the waters, flash the lightnings, weigh the Sun.

O, I see the crescent promise of my spirit hath not set.
Ancient founts of inspiration well thro' all my fancy yet.

Howsoever these things be, a long farewell to Locksley Hall!
Now for me the woods may wither, now for me the roof-tree fall. 190

Comes a vapour from the margin, blackening over heath and holt,
Cramming all the blast before it, in its breast a thunderbolt.

Let it fall on Locksley Hall, with rain or hail, or fire or snow;
For the mighty wind arises, roaring seaward, and I go.

Locksley Hall Sixty Years After

Late, my grandson! half the morning have I paced these sandy tracts,
Watch'd again the hollow ridges roaring into cataracts,

Wander'd back to living boyhood while I heard the curlews call,
myself so close on death, and death itself in Locksley Hall.

So—your happy suit was blasted—she the faultless, the divine;
And you liken—boyish babble—this boy-love of yours with mine.

I myself have often babbled doubtless of a foolish past;
Babble, babble; our old England may go down in babble at last.

'Curse him!' curse your fellow-victim? call him dotard in your rage?
Eyes that lured a doting boyhood well might fool a dotard's age.

Jilted for a wealthier! wealthier? yet perhaps she was not wise;
I remember how you kiss'd the miniature with those sweet eyes.

In the hall there hangs a painting—Amy's arms about my neck—
Happy children in a sunbeam sitting on the ribs of wreck.

In my life there was a picture, she that clasp'd my neck had flown;
I was left within the shadow sitting on the wreck alone.

Yours has been a slighter ailment, will you sicken for her sake?
You, not you! your modern amourist is of easier, earthlier make.

10

Amy loved me, Amy fail'd me, Amy was a timid child;
But your Judith—but your worldling—*she* had never driven
    me wild.

She that holds the diamond necklace dearer than the golden
    ring,
She that finds a winter sunset fairer than a morn of Spring.

She that in her heart is brooding on his briefer lease of life,
While she vows 'till death shall part us,' she the would-be-
    widow wife.

She the worldling born of worldlings—father, mother—be
    content,
Ev'n the homely farm can teach us there is something in
    descent.

Yonder in that chapel, slowly sinking now into the ground,
Lies the warrior, my forefather, with his feet upon the hound.

Cross'd! for once he sail'd the sea to crush the Moslem in his
    pride;
Dead the warrior, dead his glory, dead the cause in which he
    died.

Yet how often I and Amy in the mouldering aisle have stood,
Gazing for one pensive moment on that founder of our blood.

There again I stood to-day, and where of old we knelt in
    prayer,
Close beneath the casement crimson with the shield of
    Locksley—there,

All in white Italian marble, looking still as if she smiled,

Lies my Amy dead in child-birth, dead the mother, dead
   the child.

Dead—and sixty years ago, and dead her aged husband now
I this old white-headed dreamer stoopt and kiss'd her marble
   brow.

Gone the fires of youth, the follies, furies, curses, passionate
   tears,
Gone like fires and floods and earthquakes of the planet's
   dawning years.   40

Fires that shook me once, but now to silent ashes fall'n away.
Cold upon the dead volcano sleeps the gleam of dying day.

Gone the tyrant of my youth, and mute below the chancel
   stones,
All his virtues—I forgive them—black in white above his
   bones.

Gone the comrades of my bivouac, some in fight against the
   foe,
Some thro' age and slow diseases, gone as all on earth will go.

Gone with whom for forty years my life in golden sequence
   ran,
She with all the charm of woman, she with all the breadth
   of man,

Strong in will and rich in wisdom, Edith, yet so lowly-sweet,
Woman to her inmost heart, and woman to her tender feet,   50

Very woman of very woman, nurse of ailing body and mind,
She that link'd again the broken chain that bound me to my
   kind.

Here to-day was Amy with me, while I wander'd down the
    coast,
Near us Edith's holy shadow, smiling at the slighter ghost.

Gone our sailor son thy father, Leonard early lost at sea;
Thou alone, my boy, of Amy's kin and mine art left to me.

Gone thy tender-natured mother, wearying to be left alone,
Pining for the stronger heart that once had beat beside her
    own.

Truth, for Truth is Truth, he worshipt, being true as he was
    brave;
Good, for Good is Good, he follow'd, yet he look'd beyond
    the grave,   60

Wiser there than you, that crowning barren Death as lord
    of all,
Deem this over-tragic drama's closing curtain is the pall!

Beautiful was death in him, who saw the death, but kept the
    deck,
Saving women and their babes, and sinking with the sinking
    wreck,

Gone for ever! Ever? no—for since our dying race began,
Ever, ever, and for ever was the leading light of man.

Those that in barbarian burials kill'd the slave, and slew the
    wife
Felt within themselves the sacred passion of the second life.

Indian warriors dream of ampler hunting grounds beyond
    the night;

Ev'n the black Australian dying hopes he shall return, a
  white.

Truth for truth, and good for good! The Good, the True,
  the Pure, the Just—
Take the charm 'For ever' from them, and they crumble
  into dust.

Gone the cry of 'Forward, Forward,' lost within a growing
  gloom;
Lost, or only heard in silence from the silence of a tomb.

Half the marvels of my morning, triumphs over time and
  space,
Staled by frequence, shrunk by usage into commonest
  commonplace!

'Forward' rang the voices then, and of the many mine was
  one.
Let us hush this cry of 'Forward' till ten thousand years have
  gone.

Far among the vanish'd races, old Assyrian kings would flay
Captives whom they caught in battle—iron-hearted victors
  they.

Ages after, while in Asia, he that led the wild Moguls,
Timur built his ghastly tower of eighty thousand human
  skulls,

Then, and here in Edward's time, an age of noblest English
  names,
Christian conquerors took and flung the conquer'd Christian
  into flames.

Love your enemy, bless your haters, said the Greatest of the
    great;
Christian love among the Churches look'd the twin of
    heathen hate.

From the golden alms of Blessing man had coin'd himself a
    curse:
Rome of Cæsar, Rome of Peter, which was crueller? which
    was worse?

France had shown a light to all men, preach'd a Gospel, all
    men's good;
Celtic Demos rose a Demon, shriek'd and slaked the light
    with blood.

Hope was ever on her mountain, watching till the day
    begun—
Crown'd with sunlight—over darkness—from the still
    unrisen sun.

Have we grown at last beyond the passions of the primal
    clan?
'Kill your enemy, for you hate him,' still, 'your enemy' was
    a man.

Have we sunk below them? peasants maim the helpless
    horse, and drive
Innocent cattle under thatch, and burn the kindlier brutes
    alive.

Brutes, the brutes are not your wrongers—burnt at mid-
    night, found at morn,
Twisted hard in mortal agony with their offspring, born-
    unborn,

Clinging to the silent mother! Are we devils? are we men?
Sweet St. Francis of Assisi, would that he were here again, 100

He that in his Catholic wholeness used to call the very
  flowers
Sisters, brothers—and the beasts—whose pains are hardly
  less than ours!

Chaos, Cosmos! Cosmos, Chaos! who can tell how all will
  end?
Read the wide world's annals, you, and take their wisdom
  for your friend.

Hope the best, but hold the Present fatal daughter of the
  Past,
Shape your heart to front the hour, but dream not that the
  hour will last.

Ay, if dynamite and revolver leave you courage to be wise:
When was age so cramm'd with menace? madness? written,
  spoken lies?

Envy wears the mask of Love, and, laughing sober fact to
  scorn,
Cries to Weakest as to Strongest, 'Ye are equals, equal-
  born.'   110

Equal-born? O yes, if yonder hill be level with the flat.
Charm us, Orator, till the Lion look no larger than the Cat,

Till the Cat thro' that mirage of overheated language loom
Larger than the Lion,—Demos end in working its own doom.

Russia bursts our Indian barrier, shall we fight her? shall we
　　yield?
Pause! before you sound the trumpet, hear the voices from
　　the field.

Those three hundred millions under one Imperial sceptre
　　now,
Shall we hold them? shall we loose them? take the suffrage
　　of the plow.

Nay, but these would feel and follow Truth if only you and
　　you,
Rivals of realm-ruining party, when you speak were wholly
　　true.

Plowmen, Shepherds, have I found, and more than once,
　　and still could find,
Sons of God, and kings of men in utter nobleness of mind,

Truthful, trustful, looking upward to the practised hustings-
　　liar;
So the Higher wields the Lower, while the Lower is the
　　Higher.

Here and there a cotter's babe is royal-born by right divine;
Here and there my lord is lower than his oxen or his swine.

Chaos, Cosmos! Cosmos, Chaos! once again the sickening
　　game;
Freedom, free to slay herself, and dying while they shout
　　her name.

Step by step we gain'd a freedom known to Europe, known
　　to all;

Step by step we rose to greatness,—thro' the tonguesters we
    may fall. 130

You that woo the Voices—tell them 'old experience is a fool,'
Teach your flatter'd kings that only those who cannot read
    can rule.

Pluck the mighty from their seat, but set no meek ones in
    their place;
Pillory Wisdom in your markets, pelt your offal at her face.

Tumble Nature heel o'er head, and, yelling with the yelling
    street,
Set the feet above the brain and swear the brain is in the feet.

Bring the old dark ages back without the faith, without the
    hope,
Break the State, the Church, the Throne, and roll their ruins
    down the slope.

Authors—essayist, atheist, novelist, realist, rhymester, play
    your part,
Paint the mortal shame of nature with the living hues of Art. 140

Rip your brothers' vices open, strip your own foul passions
    bare;
Down with Reticence, down with Reverence—forward—
    naked—let them stare.

Feed the budding rose of boyhood with the drainage of your
    sewer;
Send the drain into the fountain, lest the stream should issue
    pure.

Set the maiden fancies wallowing in the troughs of
    Zolaism,—
Forward, forward, ay and backward, downward too into
    the abysm.

Do your best to charm the worst, to lower the rising race
    of men;
Have we risen from out the beast, then back into the beast
    again?

Only 'dust to dust' for me that sicken at your lawless din,
Dust in wholesome old-world dust before the newer world
    begin.   150

Heated am I? you—you wonder—well, it scarce becomes
    mine age—
Patience! let the dying actor mouth his last upon the stage.

Cries of unprogressive dotage ere the dotard fall asleep?
Noises of a current narrowing, not the music of a deep?

Ay, for doubtless I am old, and think gray thoughts, for I
    am gray:
After all the stormy changes shall we find a changeless May?

After madness, after massacre, Jacobinism and Jacquerie,
Some diviner force to guide us thro' the days I shall not see?

When the schemes and all the systems, Kingdoms and
    Republics fall,
Something kindlier, higher, holier—all for each and each
    for all?   160

All the full-brain, half-brain races, led by Justice, Love, and
  Truth;
All the millions one at length with all the visions of my
  youth?

All diseases quench'd by Science, no man halt, or deaf or
  blind;
Stronger ever born of weaker, lustier body, larger mind?

Earth at last a warless world, a single race, a single tongue—
I have seen her far away—for is not Earth as yet so young?—

Every tiger madness muzzled, every serpent passion kill'd,
Every grim ravine a garden, every blazing desert till'd,

Robed in universal harvest up to either pole she smiles,
Universal ocean softly washing all her warless Isles.   170

Warless? when her tens are thousands, and her thousands
  millions, then—
All her harvest all too narrow—who can fancy warless men?

Warless? war will die out late then. Will it ever? late or soon?
Can it, till this outworn earth be dead as yon dead world the
  moon?

Dead the new astronomy calls her. . . . On this day and at
  this hour,
In this gap between the sandhills, whence you see the
  Locksley tower,

Here we met, our latest meeting—Amy—sixty years ago—
She and I—the moon was falling greenish thro' a rosy glow,

Just above the gateway tower, and even where you see her
    now—
Here we stood and claspt each other, swore the seeming-
    deathless vow. . . .   180

Dead, but how her living glory lights the hall, the dune, the
    grass!
Yet the moonlight is the sunlight, and the sun himself will
    pass.

Venus near her! smiling downward at this earthlier earth of
    ours,
Closer on the Sun, perhaps a world of never fading flowers.

Hesper, whom the poet call'd the Bringer home of all good
    things.
All good things may move in Hesper, perfect peoples,
    perfect kings.

Hesper—Venus—were we native to that splendour or in
    Mars,
We should see the Globe we groan in, fairest of their
    evening stars.

Could we dream of wars and carnage, craft and madness,
    lust and spite,
Roaring London, raving Paris, in that point of peaceful
    light?   190

Might we not in glancing heavenward on a star so silver-
    fair,
Yearn, and clasp the hands and murmur, 'Would to God
    that we were there'?

Forward, backward, backward, forward, in the immeasur-
    able sea,
Sway'd by vaster ebbs and flows than can be known to you
    or me.

All the suns—are these but symbols of innumerable man,
Man or Mind that sees a shadow of the planner or the plan?

Is there evil but on earth? or pain in every peopled sphere?
Well be grateful for the sounding watchword 'Evolution'
    here,

Evolution ever climbing after some ideal good,
And Reversion ever dragging Evolution in the mud.   200

What are men that He should heed us? cried the king of
    sacred song;
Insects of an hour, that hourly work their brother insect
    wrong,

While the silent Heavens roll, and Suns along their fiery
    way,
All their planets whirling round them, flash a million miles
    a day.

Many an Æon moulded earth before her highest, man, was
    born,
Many an Æon too may pass when earth is manless and
    forlorn,

Earth so huge, and yet so bounded—pools of salt, and plots
    of land—
Shallow skin of green and azure—chains of mountain, grains
    of sand!

Only That which made us, meant us to be mightier by and
by,
Set the sphere of all the boundless Heavens within the
human eye, 210

Sent the shadow of Himself, the boundless, thro' the human
soul;
Boundless inward, in the atom, boundless outward, in the
Whole.

.   .   .   .

Here is Locksley Hall, my grandson, here the lion-guarded
gate.
Not to-night in Locksley Hall—to-morrow—you, you
come so late.

Wreck'd—your train—or all but wreck'd? a shatter'd wheel?
a vicious boy!
Good, this forward, you that preach it, is it well to wish you
joy?

Is it well that while we range with Science, glorying in the
Time,
City children soak and blacken soul and sense in city slime?

There among the glooming alleys Progress halts on palsied
feet,
Crime and hunger cast our maidens by the thousand on the
street. 220

There the Master scrimps his haggard sempstress of her
daily bread,
There a single sordid attic holds the living and the dead.

There the smouldering fire of fever creeps across the rotted
    floor,
And the crowded couch of incest in the warrens of the poor.

Nay, your pardon, cry your 'forward,' yours are hope and
    youth, but I—
Eighty winters leave the dog too lame to follow with the
    cry,

Lame and old, and past his time, and passing now into the
    night;
Yet I would the rising race were half as eager for the light.

Light the fading gleam of Even? light the glimmer of the
    dawn?
Aged eyes may take the growing glimmer for the gleam
    withdrawn.   230

Far away beyond her myriad coming changes earth will be
Something other than the wildest modern guess of you and
    me.

Earth may reach her earthly-worst, or if she gain her earthly-
    best,
Would she find her human offspring this ideal man at rest?

Forward then, but still remember how the course of Time
    will serve,
Crook and turn upon itself in many a backward streaming
    curve.

Not the Hall to-night, my grandson! Death and Silence
    hold their own.
Leave the Master in the first dark hour of his last sleep alone.

Worthier soul was he than I am, sound and honest, rustic
  Squire,
Kindly landlord, boon companion—youthful jealousy is a
  liar.   240

Cast the poison from your bosom, oust the madness from
  your brain.
Let the trampled serpent show you that you have not lived
  in vain.

Youthful! youth and age are scholars yet but in the lower
  school,
Nor is he the wisest man who never proved himself a fool.

Yonder lies our young sea-village—Art and Grace are less
  and less:
Science grows and Beauty dwindles—roofs of slated
  hideousness!

There is one old Hostel left us where they swing the
  Locksley shield,
Till the peasant cow shall butt the 'Lion passant' from his
  field.

Poor old Heraldry, poor old History, poor old Poetry,
  passing hence,
In the common deluge drowning old political common-
  sense!'   250

Poor old voice of eighty crying after voices that have fled!
All I loved are vanish'd voices, all my steps are on the dead.

All the world is ghost to me, and as the phantom disappears,
Forward far and far from here is all the hope of eighty years.

   .   .   .   .

In this Hostel—I remember—I repent it o'er his grave—
Like a clown—by chance he met me—I refused the hand he
gave.

From that casement where the trailer mantles all the
mouldering bricks—
I was then in early boyhood, Edith but a child of six—

While I shelter'd in this archway from a day of driving
showers—
Peept the winsome face of Edith like a flower among the
flowers.   260

Here to-night! the Hall to-morrow, when they toll the
Chapel bell!
Shall I hear in one dark room a wailing, 'I have loved thee
well.'

Then a peal that shakes the portal—one has come to claim
his bride,
Her that shrank, and put me from her, shriek'd, and started
from my side—

Silent echoes! You, my Leonard, use and not abuse your day,
Move among your people, know them, follow him who led
the way,

Strove for sixty widow'd years to help his homelier brother
men,
Served the poor, and built the cottage, raised the school, and
drain'd the fen.

Hears he now the Voice that wrong'd him? who shall swear
it cannot be?

Earth would never touch her worst, were one in fifty such
as he.   270

Ere she gain her Heavenly-best, a God must mingle with
the game:
Nay, there may be those about us whom we neither see
nor name,

Felt within us ourselves, the Powers of Good, the Powers
of Ill,
Strowing balm, or shedding poison in the fountains of the
Will.

Follow you the Star that lights a desert pathway, yours or
mine.
Forward, till you see the highest Human Nature is divine.

Follow Light, and do the Right—for man can half-control
his doom—
Till you find the deathless Angel seated in the vacant tomb.

Forward, let the stormy moment fly and mingle with the
Past.
I that loathed, have come to love him. Love will conquer at
the last.   280

Gone at eighty, mine own age, and I and you will bear the
pall;
Then I leave thee Lord and Master, latest Lord of Locksley
Hall.

Sir Galahad

My good blade carves the casques of men,
  My tough lance thrusteth sure,
My strength is as the strength of ten,
  Because my heart is pure.
The shattering trumpet shrilleth high,
  The hard brands shiver on the steel,
The splinter'd spear-shafts crack and fly,
  The horse and rider reel:
They reel, they roll in clanging lists,
  And when the tide of combat stands,   10
Perfume and flowers fall in showers,
  That lightly rain from ladies' hands.

How sweet are looks that ladies bend
  On whom their favours fall!
For them I battle till the end,
  To save from shame and thrall:
But all my heart is drawn above,
  My knees are bow'd in crypt and shrine:
I never felt the kiss of love,
  Nor maiden's hand in mine.   20
More bounteous aspects on me beam,
  Me mightier transports move and thrill;
So keep I fair thro' faith and prayer
  A virgin heart in work and will.

When down the stormy crescent goes,
  A light before me swims,
Between dark stems the forest glows,
  I hear a noise of hymns:

Then by some secret shrine I ride;
  I hear a voice but none are there;   30
The stalls are void, the doors are wide,
  The tapers burning fair.
Fair gleams the snowy altar-cloth,
  The silver vessels sparkle clean,
The shrill bell rings, the censer swings,
  And solemn chaunts resound between.

Sometimes on lonely mountain-meres
  I find a magic bark;
I leap on board: no helmsman steers:
  I float till all is dark.   40
A gentle sound, an awful light!
  Three angels bear the holy Grail:
With folded feet, in stoles of white,
  On sleeping wings they sail.
Ah, blessed vision! blood of God!
  My spirit beats her mortal bars,
As down dark tides the glory slides,
  And star-like mingles with the stars.

When on my goodly charger borne
  Thro' dreaming towns I go,   50
The cock crows ere the Christmas morn,
  The streets are dumb with snow.
The tempest crackles on the leads,
  And, ringing, springs from brand and mail;
But o'er the dark a glory spreads,
  And gilds the driving hail.
I leave the plain, I climb the height;
  No branchy thicket shelter yields;
But blessed forms in whistling storms
  Fly o'er waste fens and windy fields.   60

A maiden knight—to me is given
  Such hope, I know not fear;
I yearn to breathe the airs of heaven
  That often meet me here.
I muse on joy that will not cease,
  Pure spaces clothed in living beams,
Pure lilies of eternal peace,
  Whose odours haunt my dreams;
And, stricken by an angel's hand,
  This mortal armour that I wear,   70
This weight and size, this heart and eyes,
  Are touch'd, are turn'd to finest air.

The clouds are broken in the sky,
  And thro' the mountain-walls
A rolling organ-harmony
  Swells up, and shakes and falls.
Then move the trees, the copses nod,
  Wings flutter, voices hover clear:
'O just and faithful knight of God!
  Ride on! the prize is near.'   80
So pass I hostel, hall, and grange;
  By bridge and ford, by park and pale,
All-arm'd I ride, whate'er betide,
  Until I find the holy Grail.

A Farewell

Flow down, cold rivulet, to the sea,
  Thy tribute wave deliver:
No more by thee my steps shall be,
  For ever and for ever.

Flow, softly flow, by lawn and lea,
    A rivulet then a river:
No where by thee my steps shall be,
    For ever and for ever.

But here will sigh thine alder tree,
    And here thine aspen shiver;
And here by thee will hum the bee,
    For ever and for ever.

A thousand suns will stream on thee,
    A thousand moons will quiver;
But not by thee my steps shall be,
    For ever and for ever.

The Splendour Falls

The splendour falls on castle walls
    And snowy summits old in story:
The long light shakes across the lakes,
    And the wild cataract leaps in glory.
Blow, bugle, blow, set the wild echoes flying,
Blow, bugle; answer, echoes, dying, dying, dying.

O hark, O hear! how thin and clear,
    And thinner, clearer, farther going!
O sweet and far from cliff and scar
    The horns of Elfland faintly blowing!
Blow, let us hear the purple glens replying:
Blow, bugle; answer, echoes, dying, dying, dying.

O love, they die in yon rich sky,
    They faint on hill or field or river:
Our echoes roll from soul to soul,
    And grow for ever and for ever.
Blow, bugle, blow, set the wild echoes flying,
And answer, echoes, answer, dying, dying, dying.

The Charge of the Light Brigade

I

Half a league, half a league,
    Half a league onward,
All in the valley of Death
    Rode the six hundred.
'Forward, the Light Brigade!
Charge for the guns!' he said:
Into the valley of Death
    Rode the six hundred.

II

'Forward, the Light Brigade!'
Was there a man dismay'd?   10
Not tho' the soldier knew
    Some one had blunder'd:
Their's not to make reply,
Their's not to reason why,
Their's but to do and die:
Into the valley of Death
    Rode the six hundred.

Cannon to right of them,
Cannon to left of them,
Cannon in front of them
  Volley'd and thunder'd;
Storm'd at with shot and shell,
Boldly they rode and well,
Into the jaws of Death,
Into the mouth of Hell
  Rode the six hundred.

IV

Flash'd all their sabres bare,
Flash'd as they turn'd in air
Sabring the gunners there,
Charging an army, while
  All the world wonder'd:
Plunged in the battery-smoke
Right thro' the line they broke
Cossack and Russian
Reel'd from the sabre-stroke
  Shatter'd and sunder'd.
Then they rode back, but not
  Not the six hundred.

V

Cannon to right of them,
Cannon to left of them,
Cannon behind them
  Volley'd and thunder'd;
Storm'd at with shot and shell,
While horse and hero fell,
They that had fought so well
Came thro' the jaws of Death,

Back from the mouth of Hell,
All that was left of them,
  Left of six hundred.

VI

When can their glory fade?   50
O the wild charge they made!
  All the world wonder'd.
Honour the charge they made!
Honour the Light Brigade,
  Noble six hundred!

The Daisy

Written at Edinburgh

O love, what hours were thine and mine,
In lands of palm and southern pine;
  In lands of palm, of orange-blossom,
Of olive, aloe, and maize and vine.

What Roman strength Turbìa show'd
In ruin, by the mountain road;
  How like a gem, beneath, the city
Of little Monaco, basking, glow'd.

How richly down the rocky dell
The torrent vineyard streaming fell   10
  To meet the sun and sunny waters,
That only heaved with a summer swell.

What slender campanili grew
By bays, the peacock's neck in hue;
   Where, here and there, on sandy beaches
A milky-bell'd amaryllis blew.

How young Columbus seem'd to rove,
Yet present in his natal grove,
   Now watching high on mountain cornice,
And steering, now, from a purple cove,   20

Now pacing mute by ocean's rim;
Till, in a narrow street and dim,
   I stay'd the wheels at Cogoletto,
And drank, and loyally drank to him.

Nor knew we well what pleased us most,
Not the clipt palm of which they boast;
   But distant colour, happy hamlet,
A moulder'd citadel on the coast,

Or tower, or high hill-convent, seen
A light amid its olives green;   30
   Or olive-hoary cape in ocean;
Or rosy bloom in hot ravine,

Where oleanders flush'd the bed
Of silent torrents, gravel-spread;
   And, crossing, oft we saw the glisten
Of ice, far up on a mountain head.

We loved that hall, tho' white and cold,
Those niched shapes of noble mould,
   A princely people's awful princes,
The grave, severe Genovese of old.   40

At Florence too what golden hours,
In those long galleries, were ours;
   What drives about the fresh Cascinè,
Or walks in Boboli's ducal bowers.

In bright vignettes, and each complete,
Of tower or duomo, sunny-sweet,
   Or palace, how the city glitter'd,
Thro' cypress avenues, at our feet.

But when we crost the Lombard plain
Remember what a plague of rain;   50
   Of rain at Reggio, rain at Parma;
At Lodi, rain, Piacenza, rain.

And stern and sad (so rare the smiles
Of sunlight) look'd the Lombard piles;
   Porch-pillars on the lion resting,
And sombre, old, colonnaded aisles.

O Milan, O the chanting quires,
The giant windows' blazon'd fires,
   The height, the space, the gloom, the glory!
A mount of marble, a hundred spires!   60

I climb'd the roofs at break of day;
Sun-smitten Alps before me lay.
   I stood among the silent statues,
And statued pinnacles, mute as they.

How faintly-flush'd, how phantom-fair,
Was Monte Rosa, hanging there
   A thousand shadowy-pencill'd valleys
And snowy dells in a golden air.

Remember how we came at last
To Como; shower and storm and blast 70
   Had blown the lake beyond his limit,
And all was flooded; and how we past

From Como, when the light was gray,
And in my head, for half the day,
   The rich Virgilian rustic measure
Of Lari Maxume, all the way,

Like ballad-burthen music, kept,
As on The Lariano crept
   To that fair port below the castle
Of Queen Theodolind, where we slept; 80

Or hardly slept, but watch'd awake
A cypress in the moonlight shake,
   The moonlight touching o'er a terrace
One tall Agavè above the lake.

What more? we took our last adieu,
And up the snowy Splugen drew,
   But ere we reach'd the highest summit
I pluck'd a daisy, I gave it you.

It told of England then to me,
And now it tells of Italy. 90
   O love, we two shall go no longer
To lands of summer across the sea;

So dear a life your arms enfold
Whose crying is a cry for gold:
   Yet here to-night in this dark city,
When ill and weary, alone and cold,

I found, tho' crush'd to hard and dry,
This nurseling of another sky
   Still in the little book you lent me,
And where you tenderly laid it by: 100

And I forgot the clouded Forth,
The gloom that saddens Heaven and Earth,
   The bitter east, the misty summer
And gray metropolis of the North.

Perchance, to lull the throbs of pain,
Perchance, to charm a vacant brain,
   Perchance, to dream you still beside me,
My fancy fled to the South again.

In Memoriam

VII

Dark house, by which once more I stand
   Here in the long unlovely street,
   Doors, where my heart was used to beat
So quickly, waiting for a hand,

A hand that can be clasp'd no more—
   Behold me, for I cannot sleep,
   And like a guilty thing I creep
At earliest morning to the door.

He is not here; but far away
   The noise of life begins again,   10
   And ghastly thro' the drizzling rain
On the bald street breaks the blank day.

XI

Calm is the morn without a sound,
    Calm as to suit a calmer grief,
    And only thro' the faded leaf
The chestnut pattering to the ground:

Calm and deep peace on this high wold,
    And on these dews that drench the furze,
    And all the silvery gossamers
That twinkle into green and gold: 20

Calm and still light on yon great plain
    That sweeps with all its autumn bowers,
    And crowded farms and lessening towers,
To mingle with the bounding main:

Calm and deep peace in this wide air,
    These leaves that redden to the fall;
    And in my heart, if calm at all,
If any calm, a calm despair:

Calm on the seas, and silver sleep,
    And waves that sway themselves in rest,   30
    And dead calm in that noble breast
Which heaves but with the heaving deep.

XXVII

I envy not in any moods
    The captive void of noble rage,
    The linnet born within the cage,
That never knew the summer woods:

I envy not the beast that takes
    His license in the field of time,
    Unfetter'd by the sense of crime,
To whom a conscience never wakes;   40

Nor, what may count itself as blest,
    The heart that never plighted troth
    But stagnates in the weeds of sloth;
Nor any want-begotten rest.

I hold it true, whate'er befall;
    I feel it, when I sorrow most;
    'Tis better to have loved and lost
Than never to have loved at all.

L

Be near me when my light is low,
    When the blood creeps, and the nerves prick   50
    And tingle; and the heart is sick,
And all the wheels of Being slow.

Be near me when the sensuous frame
    Is rack'd with pangs that conquer trust;
    And Time, a maniac scattering dust,
And Life, a Fury slinging flame.

Be near me when my faith is dry,
    And men the flies of latter spring,
    That lay their eggs, and sting and sing
And weave their petty cells and die.   60

Be near me when I fade away,
    To point the term of human strife,
    And on the low dark verge of life
The twilight of eternal day.

LIV

Oh yet we trust that somehow good
    Will be the final goal of ill,
    To pangs of nature, sins of will,
Defects of doubt, and taints of blood;

That nothing walks with aimless feet;
   That not one life shall be destroy'd,
   Or cast as rubbish to the void,
When God hath made the pile complete;

That not a worm is cloven in vain;
   That not a moth with vain desire
   Is shrivell'd in a fruitless fire,
Or but subserves another's gain.

Behold, we know not anything;
   I can but trust that good shall fall
   At last—far off—at last, to all,
And every winter change to spring.

So runs my dream: but what am I?
   An infant crying in the night:
   An infant crying for the light:
And with no language but a cry.

LXVII

When on my bed the moonlight falls,
   I know that in thy place of rest
   By that broad water of the west,
There comes a glory on the walls:

Thy marble bright in dark appears,
   As slowly steals a silver flame
   Along the letters of thy name,
And o'er the number of thy years.

The mystic glory swims away;
   From off my bed the moonlight dies;
   And closing eaves of wearied eyes
I sleep till dusk is dipt in gray:

And then I know the mist is drawn
    A lucid veil from coast to coast,
    And in the dark church like a ghost
Thy tablet glimmers to the dawn.   100

LXXXVII

I past beside the reverend walls
    In which of old I wore the gown;
    I roved at random thro' the town,
And saw the tumult of the halls;

And heard once more in college fanes
    The storm their high-built organs make,
    And thunder-music, rolling, shake
The prophet blazon'd on the panes;

And caught once more the distant shout,
    The measured pulse of racing oars   110
    Among the willows; paced the shores
And many a bridge, and all about

The same gray flats again, and felt
    The same, but not the same; and last
    Up that long walk of limes I past
To see the rooms in which he dwelt.

Another name was on the door:
    I linger'd; all within was noise
    Of songs, and clapping hands, and boys
That crash'd the glass and beat the floor;   120

Where once we held debate, a band
    Of youthful friends, on mind and art,
    And labour, and the changing mart,
And all the framework of the land;

When one would aim an arrow fair,
 But send it slackly from the string;
 And one would pierce an outer ring,
And one an inner, here and there;

And last the master-bowman, he,
 Would cleave the mark. A willing ear   130
 We lent him. Who, but hung to hear
The rapt oration flowing free

From point to point, with power and grace
 And music in the bounds of law,
 To those conclusions when we saw
The God within him light his face,

And seem to lift the form, and glow
 In azure orbits heavenly-wise;
 And over those ethereal eyes
The bar of Michael Angelo.   140

XCV

By night we linger'd on the lawn,
 For underfoot the herb was dry;
 And genial warmth; and o'er the sky
The silvery haze of summer drawn;

And calm that let the tapers burn
 Unwavering: not a cricket chirr'd:
 The brook alone far-off was heard,
And on the board the fluttering urn:

And bats went round in fragrant skies,
 And wheel'd or lit the filmy shapes   150
 That haunt the dusk, with ermine capes
And woolly breasts and beaded eyes;

While now we sang old songs that peal'd
    ·From knoll to knoll, where, couch'd at ease,
    The white kine glimmer'd, and the trees
Laid their dark arms about the field.

But when those others, one by one,
    Withdrew themselves from me and night,
    And in the house light after light
Went out, and I was all alone,   160

A hunger seized my heart; I read
    Of that glad year which once had been,
    In those fall'n leaves which kept their green,
The noble letters of the dead:

And strangely on the silence broke
    The silent-speaking words, and strange
    Was love's dumb cry defying change
To test his worth; and strangely spoke

The faith, the vigour, bold to dwell
    On doubts that drive the coward back,   170
    And keen thro' wordy snares to track
Suggestion to her inmost cell.

So word by word, and line by line,
    The dead man touch'd me from the past,
    And all at once it seem'd at last
The living soul was flash'd on mine,

And mine in this was wound, and whirl'd
    About empyreal heights of thought,
    And came on that which is, and caught
The deep pulsations of the world,   180

Æonian music measuring out
    The steps of Time—the shocks of Chance—
    The blows of Death. At length my trance
Was cancell'd, stricken thro' with doubt.

Vague words! but ah, how hard to frame
    In matter-moulded forms of speech,
    Or ev'n for intellect to reach
Thro' memory that which I became:

Till now the doubtful dusk reveal'd
    The knolls once more where, couch'd at ease,   190
    The white kine glimmer'd, and the trees
Laid their dark arms about the field:

And suck'd from out the distant gloom
    A breeze began to tremble o'er
    The large leaves of the sycamore,
And fluctuate all the still perfume,

And gathering freshlier overhead,
    Rock'd the full-foliaged elms, and swung
    The heavy-folded rose, and flung
The lilies to and fro, and said   200

'The dawn, the dawn,' and died away;
    And East and West, without a breath,
    Mixt their dim lights, like life and death,
To broaden into boundless day.

C

I climb the hill: from end to end
    Of all the landscape underneath,
    I find no place that does not breathe
Some gracious memory of my friend;

No gray old grange, or lonely fold,
　　Or low morass and whispering reed,　　　210
　　Or simple stile from mead to mead,
Or sheepwalk up the windy wold;

Nor hoary knoll of ash and haw
　　That hears the latest linnet trill,
　　Nor quarry trench'd along the hill
And haunted by the wrangling daw;

Nor runlet tinkling from the rock;
　　Nor pastoral rivulet that swerves
　　To left and right thro' meadowy curves,
That feed the mothers of the flock;　　　220

But each has pleased a kindred eye,
　　And each reflects a kindlier day;
　　And, leaving these, to pass away,
I think once more he seems to die.

CVI

Ring out, wild bells, to the wild sky,
　　The flying cloud, the frosty light:
　　The year is dying in the night;
Ring out, wild bells, and let him die.

Ring out the old, ring in the new,
　　Ring, happy bells, across the snow:　　　230
　　The year is going, let him go;
Ring out the false, ring in the true.

Ring out the grief that saps the mind,
　　For those that here we see no more;
　　Ring out the feud of rich and poor,
Ring in redress to all mankind.

Ring out a slowly dying cause,
    And ancient forms of party strife;
    Ring in the nobler modes of life,
With sweeter manners, purer laws.   240

Ring out the want, the care, the sin,
    The faithless coldness of the times;
    Ring out, ring out my mournful rhymes,
But ring the fuller minstrel in.   •

Ring out false pride in place and blood,
    The civic slander and the spite;
    Ring in the love of truth and right,
Ring in the common love of good.

Ring out old shapes of foul disease;
    Ring out the narrowing lust of gold;   250
    Ring out the thousand wars of old,
Ring in the thousand years of peace.

Ring in the valiant man and free,
    The larger heart, the kindlier hand;
    Ring out the darkness of the land,
Ring in the Christ that is to be.

CXIX

Doors, where my heart was used to beat
    So quickly, not as one that weeps
    I come once more; the city sleeps;
I smell the meadow in the street;   260

I hear a chirp of birds; I see
    Betwixt the black fronts long-withdrawn
    A light-blue lane of early dawn,
And think of early days and thee,

And bless thee, for thy lips are bland,
  And bright the friendship of thine eye;
  And in my thoughts with scarce a sigh
I take the pressure of thine hand.

CXXVI

Love is and was my Lord and King,
  And in his presence I attend   270
  To hear the tidings of my friend,
Which every hour his couriers bring.

Love is and was my King and Lord,
  And will be, tho' as yet I keep
  Within his court on earth, and sleep
Encompass'd by his faithful guard,

And hear at times a sentinel
  Who moves about from place to place,
  And whispers to the worlds of space,
In the deep night, that all is well.   280

CXXX

Thy voice is on the rolling air;
  I hear thee where the waters run;
  Thou standest in the rising sun,
And in the setting thou art fair.

What art thou then? I cannot guess;
  But tho' I seem in star and flower
  To feel thee some diffusive power,
I do not therefore love thee less:

My love involves the love before;
  My love is vaster passion now;   290
  Tho' mix'd with God and Nature thou,
I seem to love thee more and more.

Far off thou art, but ever nigh;
    I have thee still, and I rejoice;
    I prosper, circled with thy voice;
I shall not lose thee tho' I die.

Flower in the Crannied Wall

Flower in the crannied wall,
I pluck you out of the crannies,
I hold you here, root and all, in my hand,
Little flower—but *if* I could understand
What you are, root and all, and all in all,
I should know what God and man is.

The Revenge

A Ballad of the Fleet

I

At Flores in the Azores Sir Richard Grenville lay,
And a pinnace, like a flutter'd bird, came flying from far
    away:
'Spanish ships of war at sea! we have sighted fifty-three!'
Then sware Lord Thomas Howard: ' 'Fore God I am no
    coward;
But I cannot meet them here, for my ships are out of gear,
And the half my men are sick. I must fly, but follow quick.
We are six ships of the line; can we fight with fifty-three?'

II

Then spake Sir Richard Grenville: 'I know you are no
    coward;
You fly them for a moment to fight with them again.
But I've ninety men and more that are lying sick ashore.   10
I should count myself the coward if I left them, my Lord
    Howard,
To these Inquisition dogs and the devildoms of Spain.'

So Lord Howard past away with five ships of war that day,
Till he melted like a cloud in the silent summer heaven;
But Sir Richard bore in hand all his sick men from the land
Very carefully and slow,
Men of Bideford in Devon,
And we laid them on the ballast down below;
For we brought them all aboard,
And they blest him in their pain, that they were not left to
    Spain,   20
To the thumbscrew and the stake, for the glory of the Lord.

He had only a hundred seamen to work the ship and to fight,
And he sailed away from Flores till the Spaniard came in
    sight,
With his huge sea-castles heaving upon the weather bow.
'Shall we fight or shall we fly?
Good Sir Richard, tell us now,
For to fight is but to die!
There'll be little of us left by the time this sun be set.'
And Sir Richard said again: 'We be all good English men.
Let us bang these dogs of Seville, the children of the devil,   30
For I never turn'd my back upon Don or devil yet.'

Sir Richard spoke and he laugh'd, and we roar'd a hurrah, and so
The little Revenge ran on sheer into the heart of the foe,
With her hundred fighters on deck, and her ninety sick below;
For half of their fleet to the right and half to the left were seen,
And the little Revenge ran on thro' the long sea-lane between.

VI

Thousands of their soldiers look'd down from their decks and laugh'd,
Thousands of their seamen made mock at the mad little craft
Running on and on, till delay'd
By their mountain-like San Philip that, of fifteen hundred tons, 40
And up-shadowing high above us with her yawning tiers of guns,
Took the breath from our sails, and we stay'd.

And while now the great San Philip hung above us like a cloud
Whence the thunderbolt will fall
Long and loud,
Four galleons drew away
From the Spanish fleet that day,
And two upon the larboard and two upon the starboard lay,
And the battle-thunder broke from them all.

But anon the great San Philip, she bethought herself and went 50
Having that within her womb that had left her ill content;

And the rest they came aboard us, and they fought us hand
to hand,
For a dozen times they came with their pikes and
musqueteers,
And a dozen times we shook 'em off as a dog that shakes
his ears
When he leaps from the water to the land.

IX

And the sun went down, and the stars came out far over the
summer sea,
But never a moment ceased the fight of the one and the
fifty-three.
Ship after ship, the whole night long, their high-built
galleons came,
Ship after ship, the whole night long, with her battle-
thunder and flame;
Ship after ship, the whole night long, drew back with her
dead and her shame.   60
For some were sunk and many were shatter'd, and so could
fight us no more—
God of battles, was ever a battle like this in the world before?

X

For he said 'Fight on! fight on!'
Tho' his vessel was all but a wreck;
And it chanced that, when half of the short summer night
was gone,
With a grisly wound to be drest he had left the deck,
But a bullet struck him that was dressing it suddenly dead,
And himself he was wounded again in the side and the head,
And he said 'Fight on! fight on!'

XI

And the night went down, and the sun smiled out far over
    the summer sea, 70

And the Spanish fleet with broken sides lay round us all in
    a ring;

But they dared not touch us again, for they fear'd that we
    still could sting,

So they watch'd what the end would be.

And we had not fought them in vain,

But in perilous plight were we,

Seeing forty of our poor hundred were slain,

And half of the rest of us maim'd for life

In the crash of the cannonades and the desperate strife;

And the sick men down in the hold were most of them
    stark and cold,

And the pikes were all broken or bent, and the powder was
    all of it spent; 80

And the masts and the rigging were lying over the side;

But Sir Richard cried in his English pride,

'We have fought such a fight for a day and a night

As may never be fought again!

We have won great glory, my men!

And a day less or more

At sea or ashore,

We die—does it matter when?

Sink me the ship, Master Gunner—sink her, split her in
    twain!

Fall into the hands of God, not into the hands of Spain!' 90

And the gunner said 'Ay, ay,' but the seamen made reply:

'We have children, we have wives,

And the Lord hath spared our lives.

We will make the Spaniard promise, if we yield, to let us go;

We shall live to fight again and to strike another blow.
And the lion there lay dying, and they yielded to the foe

And the stately Spanish men to their flagship bore him then,
Where they laid him by the mast, old Sir Richard caught
    at last,
And they praised him to his face with their courtly foreign
    grace;
But he rose upon their decks, and he cried: 100
'I have fought for Queen and Faith like a valiant man and
    true;
I have only done my duty as a man is bound to do:
With a joyful spirit I Sir Richard Grenville die!'
And he fell upon their decks, and he died.

XIV

And they stared at the dead that had been so valiant and true,
And had holden the power and glory of Spain so cheap
That he dared her with one little ship and his English few;
Was he devil or man? He was devil for aught they knew,
But they sank his body with honour down into the deep,
And they mann'd the Revenge with a swarthier alien crew, 110
And away she sail'd with her loss and long'd for her own;
When a wind from the lands they had ruin'd awoke from sleep,
And the water began to heave and the weather to moan,
And or ever that evening ended a great gale blew,
And a wave like the wave that is raised by an earthquake grew,
Till it smote on their hulls and their sails and their masts and
    their flags,
And the whole sea plunged and fell on the shot-shatter'd
    navy of Spain,
And the little Revenge herself went down by the island crags
To be lost evermore in the main.

The New Timon and the Poets

We know him, out of Shakespeare's art,
   And those fine curses which he spoke;
The old Timon, with his noble heart,
   That, strongly loathing, gently broke.

So died the Old: here comes the New.
   Regard him: a familiar face:
I *thought* we knew him: What, it's you,
   The padded man—that wears the stays—

Who kissed the girls and thrilled the boys,
   With dandy pathos when you wrote,   10
A Lion, you, that made a noise,
   And shook a mane en papillotes.

And once you tried the Muses too;
   You failed, Sir: therefore now you turn,
You fall on those who are to you,
   As Captain is to Subaltern.

But men of long-enduring hopes,
   And careless what this hour may bring,
Can pardon little would-be Popes
   And Brummels, when they try to sting.   20

An artist, Sir, should rest in Art,
   And waive a little of his claim;
To have the deep poetic heart
   Is more than all poetic fame.

But you, Sir, you are hard to please;
　　You never look but half content:
Nor like a gentleman at ease,
　　With moral breadth of temperament.

And what with spites and what with fears,
　　You cannot let a body be:　　　　　　　　　　　　30
It's always ringing in your ears,
　　'They call this man as good as *me*.'

What profits now to understand
　　The merits of a spotless shirt—
A dapper boot—a little hand—
　　If half the little soul is dirt?

You talk of tinsel! why we see
　　The old mark of rouge upon your cheeks.
You prate of Nature! you are he
　　That spilt his life about the cliques.　　　　　　　40

A Timon you! Nay, nay, for shame:
　　It looks too arrogant a jest—
The fierce old man—to take *his* name,
　　You bandbox. Off, and let him rest.

Milton

Alcaics

O mighty-mouth'd inventor of harmonies,
O skill'd to sing of Time or Eternity,
　　God-gifted organ-voice of England,
　　　　Milton, a name to resound for ages;
Whose Titan angels, Gabriel, Abdiel,
Starr'd from Jehovah's gorgeous armouries,

Tower, as the deep-domed empyrëan
    Rings to the roar of an angel onset—
Me rather all that bowery loneliness,
The brooks of Eden mazily murmuring,
    And bloom profuse and cedar arches
        Charm, as a wanderer out in ocean,
Where some refulgent sunset of India
Streams o'er a rich ambrosial ocean isle,
    And crimson-hued the stately palm-woods
        Whisper in odorous heights of even.

To Virgil

*Written at the request of the Mantuans for the
nineteenth centenary of Virgil's death*

I

Roman Virgil, thou that singest
    Ilion's lofty temples robed in fire,
Ilion falling, Rome arising,
    wars, and filial faith, and Dido's pyre;

II

Landscape-lover, lord of language
    more than he that sang the Works and Days,
All the chosen coin of fancy
    flashing out from many a golden phrase;

III

Thou that singest wheat and woodland,
    tilth and vineyard, hive and horse and herd;   10
All the charm of all the Muses
    often flowering in a lonely word;

Poet of the happy Tityrus
    piping underneath his beechen bowers;
Poet of the poet-satyr
    whom the laughing shepherd bound with flowers;

V

Chanter of the Pollio, glorying
    in the blissful years again to be,
Summers of the snakeless meadow,
    unlaborious earth and oarless sea;   20

VI

Thou that seëst Universal
    Nature moved by Universal Mind;
Thou majestic in thy sadness
    at the doubtful doom of human kind;

VII

Light among the vanish'd ages;
    star that gildest yet this phantom shore;
Golden branch amid the shadows,
    kings and realms that pass to rise no more;

VIII

Now thy Forum roars no longer,
    fallen every purple Cæsar's dome—   30
Tho' thine ocean-roll of rhythm
    sound for ever of Imperial Rome—

IX

Now the Rome of slaves hath perish'd,
    and the Rome of freemen holds her place,
I, from out the Northern Island
    sunder'd once from all the human race,

I salute thee, Mantovano,
    I that loved thee since my day began,
Wielder of the stateliest measure
    ever moulded by the lips of man.   40

Early Spring

I

Once more the Heavenly Power
  Makes all things new,
And domes the red-plow'd hills
  With loving blue;
The blackbirds have their wills,
  The throstles too.

II

Opens a door in Heaven;
  From skies of glass
A Jacob's ladder falls
  On greening grass,   10
And o'er the mountain-walls
  Young angels pass.

III

Before them fleets the shower,
  And burst the buds,
And shine the level lands,
  And flash the floods;

The stars are from their hands
   Flung thro' the woods,

IV

The woods with living airs
   How softly fann'd,   20
Light airs from where the deep,
   All down the sand,
Is breathing in his sleep,
   Heard by the land.

V

O follow, leaping blood,
   The season's lure!
O heart, look down and up
   Serene, secure,
Warm as the crocus cup,
   Like snowdrops, pure!   30

VI

Past, Future glimpse and fade
   Thro' some slight spell,
A gleam from yonder vale,
   Some far blue fell,
And sympathies, how frail,
   In sound and smell!

VII

Till at thy chuckled note,
   Thou twinkling bird,
The fairy fancies range,
   And, lightly stirr'd,   40
Ring little bells of change
   From word to word.

137

For now the Heavenly Power
  Makes all things new,
And thaws the cold, and fills
  The flower with dew;
The blackbirds have their wills,
  The poets too.

Prefatory Poem to My Brother's Sonnets

Midnight, June 30, 1879

I

Midnight—in no midsummer tune
The breakers lash the shores:
The cuckoo of a joyless June
Is calling out of doors:

And thou hast vanish'd from thine own
To that which looks like rest,
True brother, only to be known
By those who love thee best.

II

Midnight—and joyless June gone by,
And from the deluged park   10
The cuckoo of a worse July
Is calling thro' the dark:

But thou art silent underground,
And o'er thee streams the rain,
True poet, surely to be found
When Truth is found again.

And, now to these unsummer'd skies
The summer bird is still,
Far off a phantom cuckoo cries
From out a phantom hill;   20

And thro' this midnight breaks the sun
Of sixty years away,
The light of days when life begun,
The days that seem to-day,

When all my griefs were shared with thee,
As all my hopes were thine—
As all thou wert was one with me,
May all thou art be mine!

'Frater Ave Atque Vale'

Row us out from Desenzano, to your Sirmione row!
So they row'd, and there we landed—'O venusta Sirmio!'
There to me thro' all the groves of olive in the summer glow,
There beneath the Roman ruin where the purple flowers grow,
Came that 'Ave atque Vale' of the Poet's hopeless woe,
Tenderest of Roman poets nineteen-hundred years ago,
'Frater Ave atque Vale'—as we wander'd to and fro
Gazing at the Lydian laughter of the Garda Lake below
Sweet Catullus's all-but-island, olive-silvery Sirmio!

Vastness

I

Many a hearth upon our dark globe sighs after many a
    vanish'd face,
Many a planet by many a sun may roll with the dust of a
    vanish'd race.

II

Raving politics, never at rest—as this poor earth's pale
    history runs,—
What is it all but a trouble of ants in the gleam of a million
    million of suns?

III

Lies upon this side, lies upon that side, Truthless violence
    mourn'd by the Wise,
Thousands of voices drowning his own in a popular torrent
    of lies upon lies;

IV

Stately purposes, valour in battle, glorious annals of army
    and fleet,
Death for the right cause, death for the wrong cause,
    trumpets of victory, groans of defeat;

V

Innocence seethed in her mother's milk, and Charity setting
    the martyr aflame;
Thraldom who walks with the banner of Freedom, and
    recks not to ruin a realm in her name;   10

VI

Faith at her zenith, or all but lost in the gloom of doubts
    that darken the schools;

Craft with a bunch of all-heal in her hand, follow'd up by
    her vassal legion of fools;

VII

Trade flying over a thousand seas with her spice and her
    vintage, her silk and her corn;
Desolate offing, sailorless harbours, famishing populace,
    wharves forlorn;

VIII

Star of the morning, Hope in the sunrise; gloom of the
    evening, Life at a close;
Pleasure who flaunts on her wide downway with her flying
    robe and her poison'd rose;

IX

Pain, that has crawl'd from the corpse of Pleasure, a worm
    which writhes all day, and at night
Stirs up again in the heart of the sleeper, and stings him back
    to the curse of the light;

X

Wealth with his wines and his wedded harlots; honest
    Poverty, bare to the bone;
Opulent Avarice, lean as Poverty; Flattery gilding the rift
    in a throne;   20

XI

Fame blowing out from her golden trumpet a jubilant
    challenge to Time and Fate;
Slander, her shadow, sowing the nettle on all the laurel'd
    graves of the Great;

XII

Love for the maiden, crown'd with marriage, no regrets
    for aught that has been,
Household happiness, gracious children, debtless competence,
    golden mean;

141

National hatreds of whole generations, and pigmy spites
    of the village spire;
Vows that will last to the last death-ruckle, and vows that
    are snapt in a moment of fire;

He that has lived for the lust of the minute, and died in the
    doing it, flesh without mind;
He that has nail'd all flesh to the Cross, till Self died out in
    the love of his kind;

Spring and Summer and Autumn and Winter, and all these
    old revolutions of earth;
All new-old revolutions of Empire—change of the tide—
    what is all of it worth?   30

What the philosophies, all the sciences, poesy, varying
    voices of prayer?
All that is noblest, all that is basest, all that is filthy with all
    that is fair?

What is it all, if we all of us end but in being our own
    corpse-coffins at last,
Swallow'd in Vastness, lost in Silence, drown'd in the deeps
    of a meaningless Past?

What but a murmur of gnats in the gloom, or a moment's
    anger of bees in their hive?—
  .   .   .   .

Peace, let it be! for I loved him, and love him for ever: the
    dead are not dead but alive.

Merlin and the Gleam

O Young Mariner,
You from the haven
Under the sea-cliff,
You that are watching
The gray Magician
With eyes of wonder,
I am Merlin,
And *I* am dying,
I am Merlin
Who follow The Gleam.   10

II

Mighty the Wizard
Who found me at sunrise
Sleeping, and woke me
And learn'd me Magic!
Great the Master,
And sweet the Magic,
When over the valley,
In early summers,
Over the mountain,
On human faces,   20
And all around me,
Moving to melody,
Floated The Gleam.

III

Once at the croak of a Raven who crost it,
A barbarous people,
Blind to the magic,

And deaf to the melody,
Snarl'd at and cursed me.
A demon vext me,
The light retreated,
The landskip darken'd,
The melody deaden'd,
The Master whisper'd
'Follow The Gleam.'

IV

Then to the melody,
Over a wilderness
Gliding, and glancing at
Elf of the woodland,
Gnome of the cavern,
Griffin and Giant,
And dancing of Fairies
In desolate hollows,
And wraiths of the mountain,
And rolling of dragons
By warble of water,
Or cataract music
Of falling torrents,
Flitted The Gleam.

V

Down from the mountain
And over the level,
And streaming and shining on
Silent river,
Silvery willow,
Pasture and plowland,
Innocent maidens,
Garrulous children,
Homestead and harvest,

Reaper and gleaner,
And rough-ruddy faces
Of lowly labour,   60
Slided The Gleam—

Then, with a melody
Stronger and statelier,
Led me at length
To the city and palace
Of Arthur the king;
Touch'd at the golden
Cross of the churches,
Flash'd on the Tournament,
Flicker'd and bicker'd   70
From helmet to helmet,
And last on the forehead
Of Arthur the blameless
Rested The Gleam.

Clouds and darkness
Closed upon Camelot;
Arthur had vanish'd
I knew not whither,
The king who loved me,
And cannot die;   80
For out of the darkness
Silent and slowly
The Gleam, that had waned to a wintry glimmer
On icy fallow
And faded forest,
Drew to the valley
Named of the shadow,

And slowly brightening
Out of the glimmer,
And slowly moving again to a melody   90
Yearningly tender,
Fell on the shadow,
No longer a shadow,
But clothed with The Gleam.

VIII

And broader and brighter
The Gleam flying onward,
Wed to the melody,
Sang thro' the world;
And slower and fainter,
Old and weary,   100
But eager to follow,
I saw, whenever
In passing it glanced upon
Hamlet or city,
That under the Crosses
The dead man's garden,
The mortal hillock,
Would break into blossom;
And so to the land's
Last limit I came—   110
And can no longer,
But die rejoicing,
For thro' the Magic
Of Him the Mighty,
Who taught me in childhood,
There on the border
Of boundless Ocean,
And all but in Heaven
Hovers The Gleam.

Not of the sunlight, 120
Not of the moonlight,
Not of the starlight!
O young Mariner,
Down to the haven,
Call your companions,
Launch your vessel,
And crowd your canvas,
And, ere it vanishes
Over the margin,
After it, follow it, 130
Follow The Gleam.

The Silent Voices

When the dumb Hour, clothed in black,
Brings the Dreams about my bed,
Call me not so often back,
Silent Voices of the dead,
Towards the lowland ways behind me,
And the sunlight that is gone!
Call me rather, silent voices,
Forward to the starry track
Glimmering up the heights beyond me,
On, and always on!

Crossing the Bar

Sunset and evening star,
  And one clear call for me!
And may there be no moaning of the bar
  When I put out to sea,

But such a tide as moving seems asleep,
  Too full for sound and foam,
When that which drew from out the boundless deep
  Turns again home.

Twilight and evening bell,
  And after that the dark!
And may there be no sadness of farewell,
  When I embark;

For tho' from out our borne of Time and Place
  The flood may bear me far,
I hope to see my Pilot face to face
  When I have crost the bar.

NOTES

Tennyson's poem is a reverie; the story of Mariana in Shakespeare's play is not at all the same. Tennyson's lonely lady is perhaps not so much the principal character of his poem as the moated grange, or farmhouse on the verge of the Fen; she is akin to his Lady of Shalott, but has less share in the whole composition. In the poem 'Mariana in the South', written later, she is still obliged to lament her solitude, and absence of lovers, but looks forward to more society perhaps in the next world.

An Ode on the subject was probably known to Tennyson in the Works of William Shenstone (of the 18th century). Its first stanza compared with Tennyson's shows the transformation of English lyricism which was the rising poet's inheritance by the year 1833:

> O Memory! celestial maid!
> Who glean'st the flow'rets cropt by time,
> And, suff'ring not a leaf to fade,
> Preserv'st the blossoms of our prime,
> Bring, bring those moments to my mind
> When life was new and Lesbia kind.

The importance of the Lincolnshire country to Tennyson's poetry is excellently expressed by him in st. iv and v.

An early instance of Tennyson's daydreams in the supposed Arthurian regions of romance. It may be conjectured that Tennyson was pleased with the mythical ladies of some recent poets, and their surroundings and stories: the Lady Christabel, the Lady of the Lake, La Belle Dame sans Merci. In his turn he fashioned this 'fairy Lady', in whose story Stopford Brooke diffidently discovered an 'interpretation'. It was that so long as the Lady was occupied with her limited world and its habitual figures, at least she was in safety; once she was attracted beyond, she was doomed. This may have been in Tennyson's mind as he presented the brilliant invasion of Sir Lancelot into her consciousness, and the deadly sequel.

38. THE TWO VOICES

The three-rhymed stanza had been lately used in his 'On my Own Album' by Charles Lamb, who admired it in Swift's poem on the Earl of Peterborough. It seems to suit a serious matter. The two voices in the mind of the supposed speaker—not necessarily Tennyson, though the dispute between hope and despair is recurrent in his work—contend over an idea of self-destruction. Here Tennyson's thinking is as deliberate and clear as anywhere in his many pages. At the end 'natural piety' wins; if the vignette of village churchgoing seems sentimental at the moment, it is not long since it was ordinary truth.

The poem ends with the word 'rejoice' exactly as does Coleridge's ode, 'Dejection'.

55. THE LOTOS-EATERS   published 1833

On his homeward voyage from Troy to the island of Ithaca, Ulysses with his men was driven by a tempest to 'a shore where a race of men dwell that are sustained by the fruit of the lotos-tree' (Homer, *Odyssey* Book IX). To continue the story according to *The Adventures of Ulysses* by Charles Lamb, 'Here Ulysses sent some of his men to land for fresh water, who were met by certain of the inhabitants, that gave them some of their country food to eat; not with any ill intention towards them, though in the event it proved pernicious; for, having eaten of this fruit, so pleasant it proved to their appetite, that they in a minute quite forgot all thoughts of home, or of their countrymen, or of ever returning back to the ships to give an account of what sort of inhabitants dwell there, but they would needs stay and live there among them, and eat of that precious food for ever; and when Ulysses sent other of his men to look for them, and to bring them back by force, they stared, and wept, and would not leave their food for heaven itself, so much the pleasure of that enchanting fruit had bewitched them. But Ulysses caused them to be bound hand and foot, and cast under the hatches; and set sail with all possible speed from that baneful coast, lest others after them might taste the lotos, which had such strange qualities to make men forget their native country, and the thoughts of home.'

Spenser having written of enchanted country in his *Faerie Queene* Tennyson employs the stanza-form of that poem; he knew also

Thomson's allegory in the same manner, *The Castle of Indolence*. To his descriptive piece he added a 'Choric Song', enlarging on the reluctance of the mariners to go back to their ordinary affairs.

Those who know the poems of Coleridge and Keats will perceive how a later Romantic such as Tennyson was haunted by their expressions.

61. OF OLD SAT FREEDOM

Tennyson renews Milton's figure of 'the mountain-nymph, sweet Liberty', and probably his poem also follows where Wordsworth's sonnet 'Two voices' refers to mountains and great waters. He places Freedom in modern England, and his 'wisdom of a thousand years' gives King Alfred a glance.

62. MORTE D'ARTHUR   published 1842

Tennyson originally produced this poem as part of a study of modern life called 'The Epic', with agreeable humour and familiarity surrounding the reading of the fragment by 'Everard Hall'—evidently himself—at a Christmas Eve gathering. The imagined epic had been in twelve books, all burnt in a critical moment as being 'mere chaff and draff' except this one. The main comment on the poem was that somehow King Arthur could come again as 'a modern gentleman', and even as a greater one than he was in the ancient world; for he might return when war should be no more. A Christmas message, not unlike that of Charles Dickens (Tennyson's admirer).

'Le Morte d'Arthur' is the title of a celebrated work in prose by Sir Thomas Malory—a dim figure—printed by William Caxton in 1485, and revived among other invaluable sources of legend and myth in the Romantic age. Tennyson liked his Malory well enough, but was chiefly concerned with him as supplying subject matter; and in the end he composed the 'Idylls of the King' without much attention to the Malory qualities. 'This inoculation of ancient stories with modern thought' is Stopford Brooke's description of his process. Modern theology, in fact, is involved in the poem or was. The 1842 poem is certainly more epic than idyllic. It bears some relation to the 'Hyperion' of John Keats.

An odd trick of the poet is the use of the word 'all'—legitimately in line 1, and 7 probably, but often merely by way of space-filling.

70. ULYSSES   published 1842

Though Ulysses was one of Homer' heroes and the central figure of Homer's *Odyssey*, it was not from that poem that Tennyson drew the precise theme of his excellent character-study. The classical Ulysses, once he had returned to his wife Penelope in his own island kingdom, made no more voyages. But after the Homeric days a legend grew up that he could not stay at home, and his imagined voyage into the Atlantic and its fatal end were described in Dante's *Inferno*, Canto XXVI; there Tennyson found his 'authority'. Incidentally, Ulysses was formerly supposed to have been the founder of Lisbon.

Concerning Telemachus, whom Tennyson leaves as ruler of Ithaca, present-day readers may consult Charles Lamb's 'Adventures of Ulysses'.

Tennyson's poem, firmer in style than much of his early work, with a manner of being translated directly from the Greek, is not only an exercise of imagination; it is also one of his utterances about his own attitude to life, which often enough in his poetry calls up a sea symbolism.

73. TITHONUS   published 1860

One more of the poems on more or less fabulous figures from ancient Greece which our European poets confidently produced in the 19th century. Tennyson's readers would know who Tithonus was, to whom wedded (Aurora), and the rest. The whole thing is crystallized in the words 'cruel immortality'.

75. LOCKSLEY HALL   published 1842

One of Tennyson's dramatic monologues: the 'I' is, of course, not intended simply for himself. The speaker—apparently walking on the sands of the Lincolnshire coast within sight of the towered Hall, on a stormy morning—is a young man embittered by a disappointment in love. He lets us know that he was an orphan, the son of an officer killed in India; he had been sent home to his guardian, the owner of Locksley Hall—his uncle. In time he had fallen in love with his uncle's daughter Amy, and she with him; but his uncle and aunt insisted on 'mating' her 'with a clown'—a monied fox-hunter, hard drinker, and generally a brute. The poem becomes partly an invective against this husband and a declaration of the speaker's interests and merits. He represents, perhaps, the young intellectuals of about 1830.

What shall he do? Retire from the civilization which by its conventions has deprived him of Amy, and marry some 'savage woman' on a South Sea Island? No; he must remain where Christianity and 'science' flourish; but he ends with a deep curse on Locksley Hall.

This narrative is curiously extended in 'Locksley Hall Sixty Years After', published in 1886. We then hear that Amy had died in childbirth, and her child with her, almost at once, and her husband had remained a widower and proved himself a really excellent squire all those sixty years. The speaker recants; and his grandson inherits the Hall; but there are still many murmurings over the spirit of the age, and recantations.

The metre (ancient Greek) has been thought to represent the incoming waves which are mentioned at the beginning; it was comparatively new in English poetry in 1842, though it was frequently employed in 'Sabbation' (1838) by Tennyson's friend R. C. Trench.

The opinions on democracy, woman, progress, China and so on may be in part or at times Tennyson's own, but may as well be taken as ingredients in the character he is composing.

105. SIR GALAHAD

The poem was the inspiration for G. F. Watts's celebrated painting, in which the knight is if possible even more saintly. There is a contrast in the poetical treatment of Galahad in the *Defence of Guenevere* by William Morris (1858). There 'the kiss of love' is not so easily passed by, and the mediaevalism is more practical; the quest of the Grail, or Sangreal, of course, goes on. To Sir Galahad alone among King Arthur's knights it was given to see this symbol.

107. A FAREWELL

The brook seen and heard in the 'Ode to Memory' is perhaps never far from Tennyson's poetry, though he may have ceased to visit his old home. He will have had in mind the verse of his master, the Latin poet Horace, concerning such streams,

> Labitur et labetur in omne volubilis aevum,

which his predecessor as Laureate adapted,

> Still glides the stream and shall for ever glide.

Modern 'development' reduces the certainty that any brook will do so, except in such poetry as Tennyson's.

108. THE SPLENDOUR FALLS

One of the songs added to the extremely Victorian metrical tale 'The Princess' in the 1849 edition. It has no particular link with the tale, but a harp with a singer playing it is supplied as part of the décor. The song may give us pictures of Lakeland, the Border country, or the Rhine (Wagner was not yet); the spirit of Sir Walter Scott may have whispered to his devotee. The importance of the words 'for ever' in mezzo-romantic poetry can be discerned here yet once more.

109. THE CHARGE OF THE LIGHT BRIGADE

An episode at Balaclava in October 1854. The British had joined the Turks against the Russians and the Crimean War was in progress. On 25 October Lord Cardigan obeyed some obscure verbal order to take his Cavalry brigade and capture Russian artillery positions of great strength. Great bravery was shown by Cardigan and his horsemen, but the Light Brigade was unlucky. Tennyson's energetic ballad was followed by his more rhetorical 'Charge of the Heavy Brigade', now unreadable.

111. THE DAISY

The stanza is probably of Tennyson's invention; he varied it slightly and cleverly for his poem 'To the Rev. F. D. Maurice'. He was some-what proud of it, thinking that he had caught 'a far off echo of the Horatian Alcaic'. 'Q' remarks with a quotation from 'The Daisy' that 'English poets have been at their best on the Riviera: from Cette where Matthew Arnold painted one of the most brilliant little landscapes in our literature, along to Genoa where Tennyson visited. . . .'

115. IN MEMORIAM

VII

The 'dark house' was no. 67 Wimpole Street, London—for many years the home of Henry Hallam, historian and father of Tennyson's friend. The poem has its contrast in CXIX, composed later on when grief had been moderated by time. The last line has been pointed out as an instance of powerful versification.

XI

Tennyson comments that this scene (from the high ground all the marsh is seen stretching to the 'main') belonged to Lincolnshire. The piece must have been written while Hallam's body was being brought home to England.

XXVII

He does not wish to be a creature without feeling, a bird that is content with its cage, an animal merely existing for its allotted time, a heart (here the metaphors are typically quaint) indifferent. 'Want-begotten rest', quietness based on some lack of ideas.

L

Discloses the darker side of Tennyson's inner, psychological inheritance. The final striking image was suggested by the lights of London.

LIV

Particularly shows the 'philosophy' which Tennyson brought into the Victorian world, disturbed by scientific genius and shaken by scepticism.

LXVII

Clevedon Church. The river Severn and the Bristol Channel in the background.

LXXXVII

Tennyson and Hallam were members of a society at Cambridge called 'The Water-Drinkers'. Hallam's rooms in Trinity College—New Court—had evidently fallen into other ownership. Michael Angelo's 'bar' seems to mean his forehead.

XCV

The place will have been Somersby, with 'the brook'. In st. i, 'the herb' is apparently grass, a Latinism; 'and genial warmth' requires some verb, 'was underfoot'. 'We' included Charles Tennyson. In st. ii, 'the board' is the dinner-table, and 'the fluttering urn' is the tea-urn. In st. iii, 'the filmy shapes' which circled or alighted are moths. In st. viii, 'Suggestion' has a sinister meaning, as in *The Tempest*:

'They'll take suggestion as a cat laps milk.'

The real Tennyson is discovered in the next three or four stanzas; the man with this strange aptness for 'something beyond'. 'That which is'—not the apparent realities of human sense. But such vision cannot be easy to record. It is ironical that the poem seems to have been regarded rather as a mystical affidavit. 'I have often', says Tennyson, 'had that feeling of being whirled up and rapt into the Great Soul.'

C

Lincolnshire landscape—his Somersby.

CVI

How neatly Tennyson works on the two meanings of 'ring out'!

The reformist in him has here spoken with little reserve; for once he even forgets to hate the French and to think battlefields are fun. Perhaps in response to a hint from Hallam's ghost he laughs at his own 'mournful rhymes'. The whole section is near the Victorianism of a great many noble spirits, who nevertheless in ordinary life had to take things as they were. In st. viii the 'darkness' is what Sara Coleridge meant when she said of Keats, 'O, he was dark'—he lacked religious light. 'The Christ that is to be', an expression that might have lost Tennyson some clerical supporters, was explained by him as 'the broader Christianity of the future', Christianism.

CXIX

The poet refers to No. VII. The 'hand' is now for him to clasp in imagination without the despair that he felt at those doors before. The very dawn is altered from the gloomy blankness of that occasion into young beauty and brightness.

CXXVI

'Love'—universal love, as in Thomson's *Seasons* and in Shelley's *Adonais*.

CXXX

A study in the idea expressed in the *Adonais* of Shelley: 'He is made one with Nature'.

126. FLOWER IN THE CRANNIED WALL

Somewhat anticipating the inquiring style of Walter de la Mare.

126. THE REVENGE

An Elizabethan episode: the fleet led by Howard and Grenville was in 1591 at the Azores awaiting the Spanish treasure fleets returning from the West and East, and the Spanish escort came along. The *Revenge*, according to Sir Geoffrey Callender, 'had been Drake's flagship against the Armada; was one of the finest battleships afloat, and quite able to stand up to several opponents at once'. Tennyson heightens the heroism of the English ship by reducing her size. The pinnace was the *Moonshine*.

132. THE NEW TIMON AND THE POETS

The title was first that of a satire published in 1846 by Lord Lytton, who included some hits at Tennyson; the reply shows how hard Tennyson also could hit when provoked.

133. MILTON: ALCAICS

Again Tennyson addresses his contemporaries, rather than us, for his world was still bred up on Latin and Greek literature. He tries his hand on a Greek stanza-form in English, and succeeds; but he had had the tune in mind since boyhood. The *Paradise Lost* of Milton is in truth not a descriptive poem, as Tennyson seems to take it, but we may applaud the special appreciation so dreamingly expressed.

134. TO VIRGIL

The problem of fame in poetry is obvious, if the poet lives long. 'Request' poems are what he is expected to supply. This is a fine one. But Virgil was a kind of Tennyson, and Tennyson describes himself and his artistic purposes while he yields his tribute to the author of the elegant epic and pleasing rural poetry of old Italy. In st. vi, the classical reader will wonder if Tennyson was, in his memory, confusing Lucretius with Virgil; but the Victorian theme is there in any case, and Tennyson has the credit as so often of voicing it.

136. EARLY SPRING   published 1885

'Come, gentle Spring! Etherial mildness, come.' So opened the great poem on *The Seasons* by James Thomson which was one of the British classics on which the boy Tennyson was brought up.

138. PREFATORY POEM TO MY BROTHER'S SONNETS

Charles Tennyson, who took the surname Turner, was a country parson, who was content to write sonnets on his village life and sometimes the affairs of the time. Many of them are admirable. He died in 1878.

139. 'FRATER AVE ATQUE VALE'

Brother, hail and farewell.

The poet Catullus was distinctly popular in Tennyson's time, and as elsewhere in his works Tennyson employs his own art most delicately upon what the ancients have left us. Nothing much happens—only, the unity of the two poets across so vast a gulf of years, located through a tour in the South.

140. VASTNESS

An example of Tennyson's willingness to present a panorama of the 19th century, somewhat as bold cartoonists like Matt Morgan did in their own medium; and when he has used his pointer as we see—surely with remarkable insight—he ends much as Matthew Arnold had done in *Dover Beach*. Love, in simplest exchange, is peace and assurance.

143. MERLIN AND THE GLEAM

A retrospect in allegorical pictures of the poet's long career. 'Q' naturally recalls Wordsworth's verses,

> The gleam,
> The light that never was on sea or land,

as he identifies Tennyson with this Merlin. The Gleam was there in *Ulysses*, and remained Tennyson's mystery to the end. In st. iii probably the misdeeds of some of Tennyson's early reviewers are remembered. The admirable metre is evidently meant to convey some impression of the ancient poetry of England, in Anglo-Saxon, on legendary matters.

147. THE SILENT VOICES

Tennyson, like Browning, is a 'difficult' man. He had *private* experiences, and might reveal a little of them in poetry—as he did in this small poem. We know from other passages in his works that the gleam of some future destiny, besides the Voices, attracted him more than immediate concerns.—The Hour seems to be the 'inevitable Hour' of Gray's *Elegy*, but so far it is at a little distance from the poet who responds.

148. CROSSING THE BAR

One more instance, the last and perhaps the best, of Tennyson's sea imagery. Its central metaphor is, of course, frequent in poetry. James Thomson, in *To the Memory of Sir Isaac Newton*, almost writes Tennyson's idea for him:

> The noiseless tide of time, all bearing down
> To vast eternity's unbounded sea
> Where the green islands of the happy shine.

The bar is the harbour-bar, or sandbank across the harbour mouth. Tennyson was on an excursion with his son Hallam when this symbol and others inspired him, and Hallam has the distinction of having been the first person to read—and to applaud—the memorable elegiac poem.

APPENDIX

Ellen Terry remembering Lord Tennyson

'I was never very ambitious,' says Miss Terry. That may have been one of the reasons why she and Irving stayed together so long. It is probably one of the reasons why she made far more friends than most actresses and was a sort of bridge that for many years linked Irving with the hearts of a small circle of mutual acquaintances. 'I believe in immortality, and my belief is strengthened with advancing years,' wrote Irving once. 'Without faith in things spiritual, this life would indeed be a weary waste.' On this side of Irving the influence of Miss Terry undoubtedly had considerable weight; and she must have lessened materially the 'dreariness' of his life by her tender solicitude and gentle worship. Tennyson's kindly admiration also, although not greatly intimate, was treasured deep in Irving's heart. He was quite touched when he recited how the dying Laureate had told his medical man that Irving would do him greater justice in *Becket* than was done for his *Promise of May*. Tennyson had hoped to write a Dante play for Irving; eventually Irving staged that dreary piece of pseudo-Italian stage carpentry by Sardou which was one of his most disastrous failures. *The Foresters* was intended for the Lyceum. Such faith had Tennyson in Irving's ability that he told him to 'do anything he pleased' with *Becket,* and the Tennyson of the Irving-Terry experience was a very attractive figure.

'Tennyson told me to say luncheon, not lunch,' says Miss Terry; and again:

'The first time I saw him he was sitting at the table in his library and Mrs. Tennyson, her very slender hands hidden by thick gloves, was standing on a step-ladder, handing him down some heavy books. She was very frail, and looked like a faint tea-rose. After that one time, I only remember her lying on a sofa. In the evenings I went walking with Tennyson over the fields, and he would point out to me the differences in the flight of different birds, and tell me to watch their solid phalanxes turning against the sunset, the compact wedge suddenly narrowing sharply into a thin line. He taught me to recognize the barks of trees and to call wild flowers by their names. He picked up the first bit of pimpernel I ever noticed. Always I was quite at ease with him. He was so wonderfully simple. . . . It was easy enough to me to believe that Tennyson was a poet. He showed it in everything, although he was entirely free from any assumption of the poetical rôle.

'That Browning with his carefully brushed hat, smart coat and fine society manners was a poet always seemed to me more incomprehensible than his poetry, which I think most people would have taken straightforwardly and read with a fair amount of ease, if certain enthusiasts had not founded societies for making his crooked places plain, and (to me) his plain places very crooked. These societies have terrorized the ordinary reader into leaving Browning alone. The same thing has been tried with Shakespeare, but fortunately the experiment in this case has proved less successful. Coroners' inquests by learned societies can't make Shakespeare a dead man. . . .

'At Freshwater I was still so young [she was seventeen and the wife of G. F. Watts] that I preferred playing Indians and Knights of the Round Table with Tennyson's sons Hallam and Lionel, and the young Camerons, to sitting indoors noticing what the poet did and said. I was mighty proud when I learned to prepare his daily pipe for him. It was a long churchwarden, and he liked the stem to be steeped in a solution of sal volatile or something of that kind, so that it did not stick to his lips. But he and all the others seemed very old. There were my young knights waiting for me; and jumping gates, climbing trees, and running paper-chases are pleasant when one is young.

'It was not to inattentive ears that Tennyson read his poems. His reading was most impressive, but I think he read Browning's *Ride from Ghent to Aix* better than anything of his own, except perhaps *The Northern Farmer*. He used to preserve the monotonous rhythm of the galloping horses in Browning's poem, and he made the words come out sharply like hoofs upon a road. It was a little comic until one got used to it, but that fault lay in the ear of the hearer. It was the right way to read this particular poem, and I have never forgotten it.'

Tennyson read his play *The Cup* to the Lyceum company at Eaton Place, and, says Miss Terry:

'Like most poets he read in a monotone, rumbling on a low note in much the same way that Shelley is said to have screamed on a high one.

For the women's parts he changed his voice suddenly, climbing up into a key which he could not sustain. In spite of this I was beginning to think how impressive it all was when I looked up and saw Edy [Miss Edith Craig, Miss Terry's daughter], who was sitting on Henry's knee, looking over his shoulder at young Hallam and laughing; and Henry, instead of reproaching her, on the broad grin. There was much discussion as to what the play should be called and as to whether the names Synorix and Sinnatus would be confused. "I don't think they will," I said, for I thought this was a very small matter for the poet to worry about. "I do!" said Edy in a loud clear voice; "I haven't known one from the other all the time." "Edy, be good," I whispered. Henry as usual was delighted at Edy's independence, but her mother was unutterably ashamed.'

INDEX OF FIRST LINES